Right Before the Bell

A Teacher's Weekly Devotional

By Jacob Way

Copyright © 2021 Jacob Way

All rights reserved.

ISBN: 979-8547634581

Right Before the Bell: A Teacher's Weekly Devotional

SOLI DEO GLORIA

To every Christian called to teach, may Christ be formed in you and your classroom.

TABLE OF CONTENTS

	Acknowledgments	13
	Introduction	16

Week 1

Day 1	Foundation of Prayer	23
Day 2	Starting with Love	25
Day 3	A Gentle Answer	27

Week 2

Day 1	Make Allies out of Enemies	30
Day 2	The Rod Redeems Folly	32
Day 3	Dying to Self, Living as Christ	34

Week 3

Day 1	Treating All Equally	36
Day 2	Benefits of Discipline	38
Day 3	Heavenly Love	40

Week 4

Day 1	Honest Feedback	41
Day 2	Seventy-Seven Times	43
Day 3	All for His Glory	45

Week 5

Day 1	Respect Begets Respect	50
Day 2	Morning and Nightly Praise	52
Day 3	Firstfruits	54

Week 6

Day 1	The Holy Spirit as the Unifier	56
Day 2	Hearts Must Change	59
Day 3	Effectiveness and Opposition	62

Week 7

Day 1	Not "Lording Over" Students	64
Day 2	Bound	66
Day 3	Actively Pursue Good	68

Week 8

Day 1	Covert Christianity	71
Day 2	Keep Your Decrees Part 1	74
Day 3	Keep Your Decrees Part 2	76

Week 9

Day 1	Do All	79
Day 2	Cyclical Praise	81
Day 3	Value in Christ over GPA	82

Week 10

Day 1	Sacrifice Comes Second	84
Day 2	God Has Won the Battle	85
Day 3	Enjoying Parent Conferences	86

Week 11

Day 1	Recipients of Grace	89
Day 2	Created for Good Works	91
Day 3	Asking for Advice Is a Necessity	93

Week 12

Day 1	Don't Work in Vain	95
Day 2	Seeking Only the Glory of Christ	97
Day 3	Judged More Harshly	99

Week 13

Day 1	Victory Despite Failure	101
Day 2	Living Out the Power of His Promise	102
Day 3	Giving Credit Where Credit Is Due	104

Week 14

Day 1	Defend the Weak	106
Day 2	Pray to Thrive, Not Survive	108
Day 3	Use Your Gift	110

Week 15

Day 1	Teaching Unconditional Love	111
Day 2	Be Mindful of Every Word	114
Day 3	The Action of Love	115

Week 16

Day 1	We Are Confined, but He Is Not	118
Day 2	Tool in the Hand of the Master	120
Day 3	Leading in the Storm	122

Week 17

Day 1	Simplicity of the Gospel Part 1	124
Day 2	Simplicity of the Gospel Part 2	126
Day 3	Simplicity of the Gospel Part 3	128

Week 18

Day 1	Work Out	130
Day 2	Equality	132
Day 3	Raised to Life	133
	Last Day of the Semester: Meditate on the Lord	135

Week 19

Day 1	Not Innocent but Ignorant	137
Day 2	Jesus: The Greater Passion	139

| Day 3 | God's Timing, God's Strength | 141 |

Week 20

Day 1	Paradigm Shift	143
Day 2	The Lord Determines Our Steps	145
Day 3	Never Give Up	147

Week 21

Day 1	Talking	148
Day 2	Clothed in Humility	150
Day 3	Play Your Part	152

Week 22

Day 1	Messianic Obedience	154
Day 2	Blessed Forgiveness	156
Day 3	A Sustaining Word	157

Week 23

| Day 1 | The Stress of My Students' Salvation Part 1 | 159 |
| Day 2 | The Stress of My Students' Salvation Part 2 | 161 |

Day 3	The Stress of My Students' Salvation Part 3	163

Week 24

Day 1	Joy from the Lord	165
Day 2	Truth About Complaining	166
Day 3	Be Grateful	168

Week 25

Day 1	Impactful Advice I Don't Remember	169
Day 2	God's Kingdom Will Succeed	172
Day 3	Our Perseverance Is a Witness	174

Week 26

Day 1	Modeling Christian Confrontation	175
Day 2	I Always Need Him	177
Day 3	Tutoring Time	179

Week 27

Day 1	We Submit Because We Love Him	181

| Day 2 | Suffering Now, Glory Ahead | 183 |
| Day 3 | The Blind Wisdom of Fools | 185 |

Week 28

Day 1	Spiritual Battle Alongside Students Part 1	188
Day 2	Spiritual Battle Alongside Students Part 2	190
Day 3	Spiritual Battle Alongside Students Part 3	192

Week 29

Day 1	Spiritual Battle Alongside Students Part 4	194
Day 2	Sow Indiscriminately	196
Day 3	Lives Worthy	197

Week 30

Day 1	Seeing Growth and Fruit	199
Day 2	Holy, Not Happy	201
Day 3	A Needed Reminder	204

Week 31

Day 1	Apologizing for Gossip	205
Day 2	We Are Made Strong to Help Others	207
Day 3	God's Plan Is Often Counter to Our Plan	209

Week 32

Day 1	Never Stop Humbling Yourself by Apologizing	211
Day 2	Simple Evangelism	214
Day 3	Who the Son Sets Free	216

Week 33

Day 1	Standing Firm, Even if You Are Alone	219
Day 2	In Hindsight, God Is Working	222
Day 3	We Are Not the Conductor but a Stop Along Students' Journeys	224
	Last Day of School: Final Prayer	226
	Final Thoughts	228
	About the Author	229

ACKNOWLEDGMENTS

I am nothing without my Lord and Savior, Jesus Christ. By His sacrificial love, He has purchased me for Himself. I was made by Him and for Him. In Him, I find my identity, value, joy, and eternal life. Though I fail Him daily, He has never let me down or failed me. His love compels me to live every day with Him and for Him. May He be made famous by my life.

This book would also not be possible without my incredible and loving wife, Rachel. When I first approached her saying that I thought the Lord was calling me to write a book, she didn't even hesitate and told me I could do it. She has always encouraged me. Especially when I have been down and tired, she always championed this project. She has also patiently given me the time to write this book. I spent countless nights in my office and many hours in coffee shops on the weekend frantically typing away. All the while, she has believed in me and this book from the very beginning to the end. Without her steadfast support, I would have given up years ago.

My parents and sister have also been a bedrock of support. I could never thank my parents enough for loving me and raising me in the Church. I was given the blessing of a Christian foundation that prioritized God above all other commitments and distractions. My mom and dad also took the time to help me to improve this book. Their commitment to me as loving parents knows no bounds.

I must also include appreciation for my extended family. They have also been committed to me and encouraging throughout all parts of this process. I am truly blessed to be part of a family no matter which house I visit on holidays.

I am deeply indebted to Dr. Jonathan Lux. His editing not only improved my manuscripts, but his perspective and insight helped give this book its focus. He helped me pull the weeds so that the flowers could be seen better.

Amy Krause was also instrumental in bringing this book to completion. She corrected mistakes that immensely improved the clarity and quality of this book. She not only edited but also formatted and standardized every page. Her professionalism polished this work beyond what I could have ever done.

I am also thrilled to have the cover design and page layouts done by Lauren Shoemaker. She accurately captured the tone and message of the book while making it appealing. I highly recommend her for any graphic design work; she is incredibly competent and helpful.

Lastly, I want to say a special thank you to all of my colleagues and administrators, both past and present.

Without your support and belief in me, I never would have made it as a teacher. Thank you for all you have done for me and students around the world.

INTRODUCTION

I cannot say with any amount of confidence when the idea for this book began.

I suppose the thought came to me when I was wrapping up my student teaching in April of 2013. I remember the breadth of my naivety. I thought that my study of Piaget, my incredible PowerPoint skills, and my research paper on classroom management would bring principals to their knees, begging me to work for them. Besides, because of my overkill ten-page lesson plans, the school board would work a budgetary miracle and pay me 50% over the state minimum salary to reward me for being such a great teacher.

I was invincible. My future principal might as well award me "Teacher of the Year."

Sigh.

If only I were kidding.

Instead, when I first entered my classroom, I walked into reality. I quickly discovered that PowerPoint didn't run well on our new digital boards. I was not quizzed on Piaget, and the only instruction I received about classroom management was where the panic button was located and when to press it. My principal was supportive and incredibly grateful to me, but I was paid the same as every first-year teacher. All of my theories and idealism were confronted with the practical realism of teaching.

As I reflect on the beginning of my education career, I realize that I had lots of head knowledge about teaching but not so much on what matters most. My real mission, my true purpose, was to be salt and light in a dark world and point my students to Jesus. But how do you do that? Sure, I could take apart a state standard and write a great objective statement, but what about my real purpose? How do I teach as a Christian?

Perhaps the idea for this book came to me the first week of teaching when I was taking roll and had a student scream and try to fight the student in front of him for no apparent reason. I stood there in shock, wanting to escape the nightmare.

I remember thinking, "I must be a terrible teacher if I haven't even made it through the R's, and a fight almost broke out." How was I to handle such a situation? What would Piaget do? Maybe my PowerPoint would convince these kids to calm down so that I could continue with my life-changing lesson.

Sigh.

Perhaps the idea for this book manifested itself when my heart broke as a tearful student opened up to me about the challenges of her home life. I looked over all 1,400 words of my detailed lesson plan and couldn't find what to do or say.

Sigh.

Man, this teaching thing is so much more than I realized.

What does God say about being a teacher?

How can I best manage a classroom in a God-honoring way?

How can I make the most of my mission field and get the most satisfaction in fulfilling my purpose?

How does my identity as a Christian impact my classroom?

How does my faith relate to my profession?

And how will my profession impact my faith?

I spent months looking for a book that would answer these questions but could never find it.

I asked the Lord these questions, and He was patient and gracious to me. Slowly but surely, He began giving me the answers.

Perhaps that is when the idea for this book came about. When I began to seek Him, He began to open up the Scriptures and pour out His wisdom in my life. These truths and principles naturally began to flow into my classroom. The more questions I asked, the more answers He provided.

This book comprises my eight-year journey of looking to the Scriptures through the eyes of a teacher. In just eight years, I have taught on the extreme ends of education. For the first four years, I taught in a Title I public school in Texas. Ninety percent of our students were at or below the national poverty line. Free and reduced lunch and federal aid programs were essential to the life of our school. You can imagine the multifaceted difficulties that poverty includes for the social and educational life of our students. Many students came from a single-parent home, and if they were the eldest child, they routinely cooked and cleaned for their younger siblings. We were also a minority-majority school split with 50% African-American students and 50% Hispanic-American. Our students faced an uphill battle in education. Most students arrived in high school two years below the expected reading level.

Consequently, we were the most underperforming school in our district. Every nine weeks, we had professional development and district initiatives to increase our test scores so that the federal government wouldn't shut the school down. Some of our students were first-generation high school graduates, and almost all of them would be first-generation college graduates. I had the privilege of teaching incredible, generation-changing students and I've never been surrounded by a more dedicated and hardworking faculty.

For the next four years, I left the United States and taught in the opposite environment. I taught in a private, Christian, international preparatory school. The tuition to attend our school surpasses most public universities in the States. The students are almost all of Asian descent, with a majority being Korean. They are not the first in their family to graduate high school, and college is the expectation and the norm. They routinely apply and get into the top universities around the world. They come from wealth and will probably maintain a high-level income after they graduate. They are model students who excel at schoolwork. They always beat the US and global averages in AP scores and score in the upper percentiles in the ACT and SAT. Here I also had the joy of teaching world-changing students with an incredible group of friends and faculty.

Despite these vast differences, I have been surprised at the commonalities. All students need to be taught by a loving teacher. All students are desperately in need of a Savior, and all students benefit from a teacher who teaches according to Scripture. No matter the students' income, ethnicity, culture, or language, the Bible is relevant to every classroom. Therefore, there is no significant difference in how I teach and interact with students, no matter what continent I'm on.

With experience that has spanned eight years, I had to resist the urge to completely rewrite some of my first entries. I seemed so immature in those early years. However, I opted to keep things mostly intact because it was in those stages that the Lord shaped me. Going back with hindsight would take away the honesty and vulnerability that the Lord utilized at the time.

It's funny: when I started writing this book, it was one thing, and now, eight years later, it has changed into something else entirely. I first wanted to write a practical and pragmatic book for young teachers. But as I matured, by God's grace, I started looking to the Scriptures not just for classroom management ideas but for comfort, for answers to more important questions, and for intimacy with God. Before, I had a narrow application of Scripture, and now I have found that I was gloriously mistaken. The Bible is so much more than a practical field guide. God's Word addresses the entire person. This book, therefore, speaks to the whole teacher.

Our lives as teachers and as Christians are often like a rollercoaster. Just like every class that we teach is unique, so are our weeks. Today is never like yesterday, and we don't know what tomorrow will look like. Our needs fluctuate, but God and His Word are always what we need. Throughout this book, you will find useful methodology and pedagogy and the application of Christ-like behavior and attitudes. But you will also find comfort for a hurting heart, humility for a prideful spirit, spontaneous praise, and encouragement to keep running the race.

Also, don't forget that every morning you wake up, God's grace surrounds you. Goodness and mercy follow you all the days of your life. You do not have to earn God's favor or love; He already pours it out unconditionally. Embrace grace. Therefore, don't read the Bible or this devotion as just rules to follow but as ways to love Christ. Love Him by obeying Him. Don't try to impress Him but serve Him out of a grateful heart for all He has done for you.

I pray that this devotion will be of some use to you but ultimately may it magnify and direct all glory to God. I pray you apply these devotions to your personal and professional life and that, by doing so, you find ways to glorify God in your classroom.

Thank you for being the conscientious teacher that you are. Your students are already blessed beyond measure to have you in the classroom. You were specifically gifted and called to be the teacher for your students. Don't ever forget that they are why you chose this career.

I pray that your school year is better than last year and that the God of peace will do things through you greater than you can possibly think or imagine.

- Jacob Way 2021

Week 1 Day 1

Foundation of Prayer

Do not be anxious about anything, but in everything by prayer and supplication with thanksgiving let your requests be made known to God.
Proverbs 4:6 (ESV)

The first day of school is finally here! You stayed up late cutting out the perfect decorations for your room, the desks are ideally arranged, and you have written your name superbly on the board. Regardless of your level of experience, nothing quite compares to the excitement of the first day of school. On this day, it is easy to remember to pray for yourself. However, I want to encourage you to pray specifically and intentionally over each future student. I like to do this by either praying through my roster or praying over each desk. I will pray for different things as the Spirit leads me. As an example, I will pray for healing for this student, for this student to understand God's grace, for me to have incredible patience for this student, and maybe a moment to share the Gospel with this student, and so on.

Pray for whatever the Lord brings to your heart as you walk and hover over each desk. If the Lord doesn't bring anything specific, then pray that a strong rapport is built and that this student will clearly see Jesus in your daily actions.

I am overwhelmed by how faithful God is to answer these prayers throughout the school year. Later in the year, I will have a powerful, Spirit-filled conversation with a student. Afterward, I will wonder what prompted that talk, and then the Lord reminds me that the foundation of the year was laid in prayer.

It can be very nerve-wracking starting the first day of school. Your roster is filled with kids whose hearts you don't know yet. But take confidence that God has assembled your roster. Be comforted that these next 180 days were planned before the world was formed.

Take a deep breath and pray. He is with you and will be with you every day this year.

Pray for whatever comes to your heart.

Week 1 Day 2
Starting With Love

That you, being rooted and grounded in love, may have strength to comprehend with all the saints what is the breadth and length and height and depth, and to know the love of Christ that surpasses knowledge.
Ephesians 3:17-19 (ESV)

Day two of the school year: the universal day to explain the syllabus you gave students as they ran out the door yesterday. The temptation to skip explaining expectations is strong, but you cannot give in. It is crucial that today you elaborate on how the classroom will run. I always start and end with respect. I explain to my students that I will always give them respect and therefore demand it in return. I reinforce this throughout the year by addressing students as Mr. and Ms. as well as "sir" and "ma'am." Another aspect of respect is high academic and social expectations. Students will only achieve as much as you require. Aim low, and they will reach low. But aim high, and you will be pleasantly surprised.

I also frame my high expectations as an act of love. I tell them that I love them and I want them to succeed in life. This means that I will hold them to high expectations. Explaining to students that you care for them and are not against them at the beginning of the year helps build meaningful rapport. By laying the relational foundation in unconditional love, trust is gained. All of our students desperately crave security in relationships. This trust shortens the timeframe for meaningful connections and strengthens rapport with students.

The most important lesson today is that students leave knowing they are unconditionally loved and supported by you. A class rooted in love is a drop of water that can point our students to the ocean of God's love. Pray the Lord gives you the words, delivery, and tone in describing your expectations. This talk can serve as an incredible foundation for the relationship to be built on. Therefore, pray believing that the Lord will bring this conversation to you and your students' minds throughout the year.

Unconditional love

Week 1 Day 3

A Gentle Answer

A gentle answer turns away wrath, but a harsh word stirs up anger.
Proverbs 15:1 (NIV)

I remember when my second semester of teaching began. I was excited. Recharged from Christmas break and feeling a tad more confident in my abilities, I knew that my classroom management would only continue to improve.

Then he walked in.

Yes, that student. The one who is in trouble so often that you forget he is on the roll, and when he does show up, he doesn't stay in class the whole forty-five minutes.

Yes, him.

He walks in, and when the bell rings, he remains standing up. My soaring confidence plummets to the floor.

I ask him to take his assigned seat like everyone else and begin his bellringer.

He stares me in the eye and says, "No."

I gulp. I try again, this time being both firm and sly. I

say, "I know you weren't here last month, but we all got new seating charts, and I've been saving your new seat for you. Now you just have to claim it."

No." Rage all of a sudden seems to well up inside of him, and he shakes and screams, "You can't do anything to me, Mr. Way! I've been to prison!"

What should I say? His tone cannot be tolerated, and if I don't act soon, all of my authority will be gone with the rest of the class. I have to put him in his place. I have to break him. I have to match his level of anger with a level of my authority.

But at this moment, the Lord brings the above verse to mind, and I say the most neutral answer that comes to my head.

I look at him, shrug my shoulders, and say matter-of-factly, "You're right. I've never been to prison, but I know I can't make you do anything like they can."

Did I really just say that? Did I just state the obvious? How is that a response? What to do now?

I break eye contact, quickly trying to come up with a way to discipline him when I hear him say, "Yeah . . . good . . . okay."

He then sits in his seat, pulls out a pencil, and starts answering the bellringer.

I try to hide my shock and proceed with the class. He stays in class the whole time without an interruption.

After the day ended, I kept reflecting and wondering how that situation was diffused so quickly. It couldn't have been what I said. How was he so compliant? I realized it is true what the Lord says about wrath being turned away by a soft answer. It wasn't the words I said; it was how I said them. It was the Holy Spirit restraining me and giving me peace that broke a tense situation.

I'm so grateful that I did not need to pursue further disciplinary action that day. Firstly, because I don't know what I would have done and secondly, because I know that whatever I did, it would not have ended well.

Surprisingly, I had no other issues with this student for the remainder of the year, and he graduated! He was the first one in his family to do so—I was so proud of him. He even shook my hand at graduation. It was a happy ending to a bizarre situation.

Angrily responding to anger will only beget more anger. Truly, a gentle answer turns away wrath.

Week 2 Day 1
Make Allies Out of Enemies
When a man's ways are pleasing to the LORD, He makes even his enemies to be at peace with him.
Proverbs 16:7 (NASB1995)

One thing that always surprises me is how consistent students are. After they leave your class, another student with a similar personality comes in the next year. I found this to be true with what I call the "Alpha Syndrome." Alpha Syndrome is when a student challenges and defies you to wrestle control and authority away from you for himself/herself. You must nip this behavior in the bud initially so that it doesn't blossom into a full-blown authority crisis in six weeks. I was always nervous about having this confrontation until I saw a video on it, and the Lord encouraged me with Scripture.

So, what do you do? First, you must have a face-to-face discussion with the student on your expectations and explain why their current behavior is unacceptable. It is essential not to have this conversation in front of the whole class but one-on-one. The first time I had this conversation, I asked the student to stay after class. I made sure that the first things I said to him were genuine compliments. I pointed out his leadership and charismatic qualities. I then told him that I needed his help to keep the class on the right track for the remainder of the year. I needed him to be an example since so many of his peers looked up to him. I asked him to help me. To my surprise, he agreed to our arrangement and didn't complain one bit. I only needed to redirect him a few times throughout the year, but he held up his end of the agreement. I'm still shocked that a difficult power struggle was resolved so quickly.

I learned a valuable lesson: students are still people. When you speak with them honestly and openly, they may surprise you. Don't forget to be diplomatic with your students. They are never entirely against you, and if you can, make students your allies and not your enemies.

Week 2 Day 2
The Rod Redeems Folly
Folly is bound up in the heart of a child, but the rod of discipline will drive it far away.
Proverbs 22:15 (NIV)

About this time in the new school year, my students drop the "first week of school good behavior" and reveal their true natures. Homework gets neglected, and kids begin to challenge the discipline established the past week. Often, some of the most significant tests of my authority in the classroom happen around this time.

It is important to remember two things: First, these students are still children; even a nineteen-year-old senior is still a child at heart. They don't have the maturity, perspective, or life experience to be anything other than kids. With their age comes a certain amount of folly. Even if they come from great parents, they still think and do stupid things sometimes.

Second, the "rod of discipline" is ours to wield. Scripture reminds us that the only way for children to mature and grow up is to be disciplined. The rod we use is not a physical rod but a way to guide and correct. As a shepherd would gently steer his sheep if it were walking off a cliff, so must we correct and speak the truth when we see our students heading astray. We cannot shirk this responsibility, for, without discipline, your students will remain ignorant and fall into greater danger in the future. Continue with calm and measured discipline and praise the

Lord for such a tremendous responsibility.

Week 2 Day 3
Dying to Self, Living as Christ

I have been crucified with Christ and I no longer live, but Christ lives in me. The life I now live in the body, I live by faith in the Son of God, who loved me and gave himself for me.
Galatians 2:20 (NIV)

There is so much truth packed into this verse about our identity.

We identify with Christ in His death. In fact, we die with Him. All that we were—our rebellious nature, our slavery to sin—all died with Christ.

With Jesus, we are not a better version of ourselves but a new creation altogether. We, our old identity, no longer lives, but Christ lives in us. This means that every interaction with students, staff, and parents is a chance for them to interact with Jesus. Every word I say and every relationship is that much more consequential. What an honor and what a humbling thought.

What would Jesus do is only the beginning. How would Jesus teach, discipline, lead students, interact with coworkers—the list goes on. This means we have to die to preferences. Our regular habits and thoughts are replaced by those of Jesus. If I am naturally shy and would rather not greet students at my door, I must remember that Christ lives in me, and I must modify my behavior. Instead, I need to show my students the welcoming love of Christ each day. If I am predisposed to want to be liked and to please others, I must remember that Christ only aimed to please His Father. If I'm starting to get lazy, I remember that Christ worked until His job was complete. And if I'm too busy to pray, then I need to remember that Christ made time in the early morning to talk with His Father.

We have died, and Christ now lives in us. To live this way would be impossible without His help, and that's why the second half of the verse gives us hope and encouragement. Our new life is lived by faith and not effort. We put our trust in Him, and He will move on our behalf. Also, He moves despite our weakness. We don't have to have perfect interactions but simply put our faith in Christ, and He will intercede throughout the day on our behalf.

Consequently, His help is not based on our performance. We don't have to earn His favor or help. God already demonstrated His love for us, that while we were still sinners, He died for us. God loved you and me and gave Himself for us. This means that His love for us was His motivation for dying on our behalf. His blood seals this new life that we live in Christ. Therefore, our new life is eternally secure.

Ask the Lord today to help you die to yourself and live as Christ. May students and administrators sense that they are in the presence of God every time they see you.

Week 3 Day 1
Treating All Equally
A false balance is an abomination to the LORD, *but a just weight is his delight.*
Proverbs 11:1 (ESV)

I came across this verse, and it completely convicted me of how I was treating some of my students.

Let me explain.

Our school had recently implemented mandatory detention after school for all students who didn't complete their homework. I had enthusiastically enforced this rule on a disrespectful and contentious student who forgot his homework. Not only did he not do his homework, but he turned it in with only his name on it—easy rule enforcement there.

The next day, a different student forgot her homework. This student was kind, hardworking, and a joy to teach. To sum it up, this student was the opposite of the previous one. Here was the dilemma: I needed to be consistent and enforce the policy for each student. Even though this girl was kind and loves my class, to let her off the hook wouldn't be fair. This decision was difficult for me, but I realized that I needed to assign her a detention as well. Even though we are only dealing with homework, there is a more important principle at play. We honor God by enforcing the rules given to us by our administration. Our classroom is an avenue in which we obey and model obeying authority to our students. Therefore, we MUST treat all students equally as far as discipline and expectations go. With each imbalance of the scales, your respect and influence decrease little by little. Not only will this damage your witness, but when we dole out biased justice, it is an abomination to the Lord.

Enforce your rules equally, keep the scales of justice even, and honor the Lord.

Week 3 Day 2
Benefits of Discipline
Do not withhold discipline from a child; if you punish them with the rod, they will not die. Punish them with the rod / and save them from death.
Proverbs 23:13-14 (NIV)

This Proverb gives an ample philosophical justification and reminder on the importance of discipline.

There seem to be two leading schools of thought. One is that discipline is needed and serves the child, and the other is that discipline can harm the child, so precautions must be taken to avoid it if possible. Educators and administrators of the latter view tend to justify not disciplining students as an act of compassion. This ranges from not enforcing dress code or grading standards to treating cheating and academic dishonesty as minor offenses, if at all. The justification for this lax discipline goes like this: "Students have so much going on that if I discipline them, they will crack from the pressure and drop out of school. They know that they have done something bad and don't need to suffer the consequences of their actions. When they are older, they will figure out how compassionate I was and will thank me for being so kind to them."

I have heard both Christian and non-Christian teachers use this explanation for their lack of discipline. This philosophy sounds kind, but in reality, it is as unbiblical as it is cruel. Scripture commands us not to "withhold discipline" and debunks the idea that students can't handle it by saying that "they will not die." Students are not so fragile that they will break if they are held accountable. That assumption is pretty condescending and patronizing.

The truth is that a student will not learn discipline out in the real world if he was never taught when he was younger. The real world's consequences will be more severe, and he will be completely caught off guard. By not preparing this student for reality, the "compassionate" teacher has condemned that student to the fate of his first mistake.

The spiritual consequences are even more severe. Students must learn that their actions, and their sin, have consequences. God is merciful but only to those who call on His name. Forgiveness can't be granted without an acknowledgment of error. Mercy can't be given if justice is not established. We must discipline to "save them from spiritual death." Discipline with understanding and compassion.

But remember that by disciplining, you are loving your students—more than you know.

Week 3 Day 3

Heavenly Love

"Do not be anxious about anything, but in everything by prayer and supplication with thanksgiving let your requests be made known to God."
Proverbs 4:6 (ESV)

The first day of school is finally here! You stayed up late cutting out the perfect decorations for your room, the desks are ideally arranged, and you have written your name superbly on the board. Regardless of your level of experience, nothing quite compares to the excitement of the first day of school. On this day, it is easy to remember to pray for yourself. However, I want to encourage you to pray specifically and intentionally over each future student. I like to do this by either praying through my roster or praying over each desk. I will pray for different things as the Spirit leads me. As an example, I will pray for healing for this student, for this student to understand God's grace, for me to have incredible patience for this student, and maybe a moment to share the Gospel with this student, and so on.

Pray for whatever the Lord brings to your heart as you walk and hover over each desk. If the Lord doesn't bring anything specific, then pray that a strong rapport is built and that this student will clearly see Jesus in your daily actions.

Week 4 Day 1
Honest Feedback
A lying tongue hates those it crushes, / and a flattering mouth works ruin.
Proverbs 26:28 (NASB)

We must give accurate feedback to students. If a student's work or behavior doesn't meet expectations, we must tell them. We need to do this in love by remembering that it is not loving to disguise the truth. Grading papers comes to mind. For example, we shouldn't tell a student who received a fifty on an essay that it was a good essay. If it was good, then how did they earn a fifty? Instead of using flattery to put a positive spin on a terrible effort, we should honestly judge the paper.

Flattery has created a false threshold of self-worth. Most students today have been told they are unique, and all the work they produce is "A" quality and should be covered in gold stars. While society says this is a positive, Scripture is clear that flattery leads to ruin. I've seen this for the straight-A student who always earns one hundreds on papers and the student who struggles to write but has been passed along through the system. We must praise our students, but we cannot mislead our students with false praise. Our praise should be genuine.

As an example, to the student who received 50% on their paper, you could say, "Your introduction and first paragraph were strong, but you didn't finish the essay. If you finish it as well as you did the first part, your grade will improve next time." This is a way to be both positive and honest without providing dishonest flattery.

Accurate feedback will produce a realistic self-image. Flattery builds a façade, a house of cards of false achievement. When this false achievement is eventually and inevitably exposed, it will utterly devastate that student. This is the ruin of flattery.

Instead, love your students by building them up in truth.

Week 4 Day 2
Seventy-Seven Times
Then Peter came up and said to him, "Lord, how often will my brother sin against me, and I forgive him? As many as seven times?" Jesus said to him, "I do not say to you seven times, but seventy-seven times.
Matthew: 18:21-22 (ESV)

A student cussed you out, ripped up his homework, and slammed the door on the way out. You have written the referral, called home, met with an administrator, and now that student has been placed in in-school suspension for two days.

Later that week, he will report back to class; now what?

This scenario is not hypothetical; it happened to me in my second year of teaching. I had three days to figure out what I would do when this student showed up on Friday at 8:15.

I was reading through Matthew and came to these verses. Then I knew what I needed to do, although I knew it wasn't what I initially wanted to do.

It would be really easy to ignore this student. Perhaps depriving him/her of attention will help make your point. Maybe ignoring them long enough will make them apologize sooner. Then, once they make the first move, the relationship can be restored.

But this is not what's best. You are an adult and a Christian. You need to make the first move. You need to reflect the forgiveness of Christ. Your kindness to them can lead them to apologize. Once they apologize, I would then challenge you to forgive, as Jesus says. Forgive, forgive, and forgive. However, many times this student has treated and continues to treat you terribly, forgive them. Regardless of the circumstances, we don't have the option as Christians to stop forgiving.

So, that Friday, I was waiting at the door to greet my student. I gave him a genuine greeting and told him I was happy to see him. You would not believe the shock on his face! He was expecting me to treat him vindictively, but grace and forgiveness totally caught him by surprise. You would not believe the transformation this had on this student. He was a different student after that day. I never had to send him to in-school suspension again, and we developed a better understanding of each other. When you forgive, you pave the way for relational restoration, and you free yourself from bitterness.

Most importantly, you will demonstrate obedience to Christ and show the type of forgiveness He grants all of us every hour of every day. Think about how much Christ has and continues to forgive you. Think of how much His kindness has changed your life—changed your eternal destination. This is the power of forgiveness. Forgiveness is transformative.

We have the privilege of genuinely demonstrating Christ to our students when we forgive them. So forgive as many times as Jesus told us: seventy-seven times.

Week 4 Day 3
All For His Glory
So, whether you eat or drink or whatever you do, do it all for the glory of God.
1 Corinthians 10:31 (NIV)

In my career, I have felt torn between the secular and religious influence that a teacher provides. Are the subjects that I teach kids valuable in light of eternity? For example, in public school, we were inundated with communicating the benefits of going to college. Every task and skill was all about helping our students get to and graduate college. Every professional development ended with some college focus, and every teacher even put a picture of their alma mater on their doors to inculcate a college-going culture. Now, this was not bad and, in fact, was necessary when teaching in a Title I school. Most of our students were on track to be first-generation high school graduates and were hoping to be first-generation college students. For them, college was a mysterious and terrifying unknown. Many grew up never dreaming of going to college; it seemed impossible. Therefore, we as a school did all we could to make college attainable and affordable. I loved all our students and wanted to do everything in my power to help them.

However, year after year of exalting college to my students left me feeling convicted. College was only four years of their life. Yes, a degree will transform their lives, but it can't save them in the end. I felt as though I was making college something more than what it is. Even if all my students got master's degrees, they would still be broken. A degree won't provide them with what their soul needs. For the first time in my life, I felt called to teach in an environment that taught about Christ. I didn't want to put bachelor's degrees above the King. This was one way the Lord led me to teach in a Christian school.

I was so confident that my new environment would help me better glorify God. Now in my classroom, I could inculcate Christian values and teach students that Christ was more precious than their GPA. Then, to my surprise, I also began to struggle. What does it mean to be a Christian teacher? Can a teacher preach all day? Christ deserves all honor and glory forever. Shouldn't I spend every waking moment with students revealing that truth to them? How can an economics lesson be better than a lesson on John 3:16? Can I find value in teaching them to write a paper well if their writing ability won't secure eternal life?

I was frustrated to find myself in the same predicament as before.

I was previously in a secular environment, limited as to spiritual impact, and now I was in a spiritual environment trying to understand the value of non-spiritual content. Then I realized that the real question I needed to answer was how can I glorify God in my classroom by what I teach? It took many months of thinking this through and asking the Lord to help sort out my heart. Then graciously, He revealed it to me.

First, God reminded me that He promised to bless the world through Israel. Even though God did not have a redeemed relationship with any other nation, He would bless them through His people. Since all believers are Abraham's spiritual children, God's promise to Abraham applies now to the Church. The Church is now an instrument to bless nonbelievers.

How do Christians bless nonbelievers? We are a blessing to others when we show them the love of Christ and help where we can. We give of our time, talent, and treasure to meet the needs of those around us. God has uniquely gifted and purposely placed His people all around the world. In this way, people can see our good works and glorify our Father in heaven. We have this incredible privilege of being His hands and feet. Whatever vocation we pursue, we serve others in the hope of seeing them repent and trust in Jesus.

This changed my perspective. I was so focused on the nature of what I was teaching and assigning it value. I only saw secular and religious topics in the classroom. I overemphasized one at the expense of the other. I thought that valuable kingdom work could only be achieved by teaching spiritual truths. I didn't believe that teaching excellent study skills was ultimately valuable. I created a division where division doesn't exist. It is not secular and sacred. God is not only glorified on Sunday mornings by worship and preaching. God is glorified by everything we do, even the mundane in our lives.

In fact, how we glorify God is not singular but all-encompassing. The verse for today is straightforward: whatever you do, do for the glory of God. Even eating and drinking can be done to reflect His worth. God is glorified when you thank Him and enjoy His good gift of excellent coffee before the first period. When you do an excellent job at cleaning out your emails, He is glorified. This means that every single action and thought in our everyday lives has eternal value. They all have spiritual significance.

With everything we do, we can honor our King. Every effort is a form of worship. You can grade papers for His glory and do afternoon bus duty for Him. You can play with your kids and love your spouse for His glory too. What an incredible privilege! Our whole lives are worship, not just Sunday mornings. This means that all that we do matters. We don't do some spiritual things and some non-spiritual things; everything is spiritual.

Consequently, it was no less important to teach organizational skills to freshmen. Freshmen need to learn how to be organized! Good organization will significantly benefit them their entire lives. Likewise, if we only focused on teaching spiritual truths, we might not be helping our students with physical needs. Sure, our students could exegete Romans, but their math scores might be so low that they can't get into college. Therefore, we can have joy and confidence in teaching well and teaching all kinds of practical, secular skills. God has ordained us as teachers to be lights and to help the world. In the act of obeying Him and loving our students, we are fulfilling our deepest calling, and our secular work becomes sacred.

The answer to the question about glorifying God is this: everything we do for the Lord is sacred, and any and every way we love our students unto the Lord is valuable. We don't have to make eternal changes to do good works and bring glory to God.

Rejoice and take heart! The Lord will use you in covert and overt ways to bless the world. Be satisfied to love your students by teaching them all that you can. In doing this, you will obey, honor, and glorify your Father in Heaven.

Week 5 Day 1

Respect Begets Respect

Do to others as you would have them do to you.
Luke 6:31 (NIV)

As the year begins, it is essential to proceed with the cornerstone of all education relationships: respect. All relationships must be nurtured with respect. If your students respect you, they will follow your directions and exceed your expectations. But how can you first gain their respect? Simple: you must show them respect. However, this is easier said than done.

I have seen and am prone to two ways of losing respect with students. First is how we speak with students. I have heard teachers lament how terrible a student is for them, and they don't know why. However, when listening to how that teacher addresses the student, the mystery is solved. Instead of talking with a student, they talk at a student. The teacher belittles, demeans, and puts down the student in class or in the hall. No one likes to be spoken to that way. I have done this countless times and had to apologize to students afterward. It is so easy to lose or not build respect by not speaking to students with respect.

We can also lose respect by how we act toward students. I have heard several teachers say, "When students disrespect me, I disrespect them. They don't deserve my respect!"

This is such a childish way of thinking and responding. You can't hold students to a standard you don't hold yourself to. We cannot stoop to that level. We need to be examples. We need to teach children how to behave. We are teachers, and more importantly, we are Christians. We imitate Christ. Can you imagine if God had that attitude with us? Before God saved us, we were nothing but disrespectful and disobedient to Him. And even after He lavished His grace on us and adopted us as heirs, we still sin and treat Him so. But He still loves us.

Christ demonstrated unconditional love to us, and what was the result? We loved and continue to love Him back. Despite our daily failings, our relationship is built and secured by His love.

I know it is challenging, but we can do the same thing with our students. If you want to have impactful relationships, you have to work at building respect. If you want your students to respect you, show them unconditional respect, and eventually, you will win them over.

Week 5 Day 2
Morning and Nightly Praise
It is good to give thanks to the LORD, to sing praises to your name, O Most High; to declare your steadfast love in the morning, and your faithfulness by night.
Psalm 92:1-2 (ESV)

Godly habits are imperative for growing in righteousness. One of my favorite practices is to praise the Lord at the beginning and end of each day. In the morning, I thank Him for His never-ending love toward me. He loved a wicked, wretched sinner with a love that will never end. Consider how amazing that is. This is not flowery language but an accurate description of the height and depth that God loves you—never-ending means that in twenty years, God will not be tired of being in a relationship with you. In five hundred years, His love for you will not decrease even one iota. And five billion years from right now, after you die and enter into His presence, He will continue to love you. Is there any truth more precious or sweet? This truth should pour out of a grateful heart and should be the first thing on our lips when we wake up.

It is also powerful to thank God for His faithfulness to us at the end of each day. In doing so, we rightly recognize His constancy and permanence in our lives. He is not distant from us. He doesn't love us from afar. He is with us and will never abandon us. No matter how sinful and fickle we are, He is faithful. Consider all the times He has proven Himself faithful to you this past week and this past year. How many difficult days did you have when it seemed like the world was against you, and He was still there to comfort you? He is faithful to His people. He always has been and always will be.

Indeed, His love and commitment to us are beyond comprehension and are always worthy of our daily praise.

Give praise to God

Week 5 Day 3

Firstfruits

Honor the LORD with your wealth and with the firstfruits of all your produce; then your barns will be filled with plenty, and your vats will be bursting with wine.
Proverbs 3:9-10 (ESV)

Firstfruits often refers to the tithe of our income. Giving to God is a discipline of our faith in which we honor God by returning His gifts to us back to Him. This helps support our local church as well as shows reverence and appreciation to God. However, the idea of firstfruits also applies to every area of our life that we are called to steward. This includes our time, talents, and other possessions. God has given us all of these resources to manage; they are not ours to keep to ourselves. This means that they do not belong to us but to Him.

I encourage you to start viewing your time in this way. We are not promised tomorrow, but the Lord has given you today. What do we do with this gift? I suggest you tithe the first part of your day to the Lord. If the first part of your day doesn't work out, then tithe the first part of your conference period. Give back to the Lord the time that He has given you. But do not just give Him only the minutes before you fall asleep or only the time walking to the copier but your firstfruits. In ancient Israel, your firstfruits were the best of what you had. When are you the most alert? When are you the most focused? Give the Lord some of that time. He deserves your best, not your leftovers. Use the time to connect with Him. Spend time in prayer, listen to worship music, rejoice, or read your Bible. I promise you, tithing your time is not only obedience but encourages intimacy with God, which is the single most excellent experience this side of heaven. When you honor Him, you may be surprised at the many other blessings He gives. When I tithe my conference period, I have even found that He will make me more productive than if I had kept all the time for me.

Honor God with your firstfruits, and He will fill your life with countless blessings, none more satisfying than more of Himself.

Week 6 Day 1
The Holy Spirit as the Unifier

And I will ask the Father, and he will give you another Helper, to be with you forever, even the Spirit of truth, whom the world cannot receive, because it neither sees him nor knows him. You know him, for he dwells with you and will be in you.
John 14:16-17 (ESV)

One of the biggest fears I had going into my first year of teaching was how I could connect with my students. Building rapport with students is critical for education in the actual teaching and the mentoring and long-term influence that we want to have. When you consider the ramifications, the task of connecting with students seems daunting and even impossible.

In my first school, I wondered how I, a white man from a middle-class upbringing, could ever connect with my African-American and Hispanic-American students in a Title I school.

What do we have in common?

By His grace, the Lord answered my prayer. Thankfully, we have a Helper who tears down walls of social division, and He connects our hearts to the hearts of our students. After a while, I could make my students laugh, and we could all talk about the same pop culture events. I started to pick up on their quirks and could read their nonverbal communication. All of a sudden, I recognized what was happening: I was building relationships with my students. I could not tell you how it happened; I know that the Lord worked in a significant way. By the end of the first semester, the Holy Spirit gave me meaningful rapport with my students and students at my school. Year after year, this remained true. New students brought different challenges, but every time the Lord helped me connect to them. For all four years at my first school, the Lord was faithful to do this. When I look back at that time, I am even more convinced that I alone could not have done this.

I am ashamed to admit it, but I quickly forgot God's provision. When I stepped into an international school with a completely different demographic than I was used to, this same fear reared its ugly head again. I started thinking, how could I reach a predominantly Asian population in a private school?

Were we so different that I was doomed never to build a relationship with my students?

The Lord quickly reminded me that it's not up to me to win this battle, He is the reason for success at my previous school, and He will show up again in my new school. What a Comforter He is! And He was faithful to me again. After a while, the same thing began to happen. The Holy Spirit gave me insight. Cultural differences began to melt away as He gave me understanding. Before I knew it, I was able to build a strong rapport with students and faculty alike.

I still don't know how it happened, but I know Who is responsible.

The Holy Spirit is your greatest asset in reaching students. He can change the heart of any student and show you opportunities to demonstrate Christ's love daily. On your own strength and in your own knowledge, you can't make connections with students. But the Holy Spirit is all-knowing and all-powerful, so this task is easy for Him. He is the ultimate unifier in your classroom. He knows each student and will faithfully grow you close to your students. Take notice of what He is doing in your classroom.

Trust Him.

Rely solely on Him.

Expect Him to show up.

Ask in faith today for the Holy Spirit to go before you and prepare your heart and the hearts of your students. Ask Him to unify your classroom and to draw students to you. You will be amazed, like I am, at His faithfulness and power.

Week 6 Day 2
Hearts Must Change

But to all who did receive him, who believed in his name, he gave the right to become children of God, who were born, not of blood nor of the will of the flesh nor of the will of man, but of God.
John 1:12-13 (ESV)

Sometimes guiding students can be so disheartening. It can feel like we labor and sow seeds and wait patiently but don't see any fruit. Other times we can see all of the steps being laid out, and students still don't take the last step of faith. Even though I know God is essential for salvation, something happens in class that makes me forget it.

I remember one class period where we were discussing if God existed. Several students were chiming in, and there was some great back and forth. Then, a student became very adamant about her atheism. She was shooting down every claim and digging her heels in on her position. A couple of Christian students tried to convince her, but she wasn't having any of it.

Then one of them started trying to share the Gospel. Sadly, they made some inaccurate claims and misrepresented the truth of Scripture instead of witnessing. Surprisingly, another atheist in the class started correcting the Christians on doctrine! He rightly explained the "Roman Road" and articulated the path of salvation. He even stated that everyone must repent and believe, and then they can become born again. They must ask for forgiveness and accept

Jesus as Lord, and then they spend the rest of their lives becoming more like Jesus. My mouth just about dropped to the floor. I could not believe this atheist knew the Scripture and the Gospel message so well.

Everyone else in the class was just as surprised, with one student even saying, "I thought you were agnostic." The student then replied, "I am an atheist, and just because I know the Gospel doesn't mean I want it; I want to live my life for me."

I was even more amazed at his answer and appreciated his honesty. But, how could a student know the Gospel and not respond? I had so much hope and then so much despair. Then, the Lord brought me to these verses. Here we see that those who believe in Christ and become children of God are spiritually born again. This brings us to the distinction of knowing the Gospel message and believing the Gospel message. All may know the Gospel, but only those regenerated by the Holy Spirit can believe the Gospel.

Consequently, this second birth is not from the will of the flesh or the will of man. Human reason cannot bring about this change, nor can someone work to earn this revelation. It doesn't matter what books you read or arguments you make; it is only by the will and through the work of God that someone can come to saving faith in Christ. This made what happened in class all make sense. This student understood the Gospel very well, but his eyes remained closed to its beauty. His heart was not softened to his spiritual condition and need for a Savior.

This reality frees us to joyfully and often clumsily share the good news, confident that its success is not dependent on us but God. I then started looking at my students differently. All of them knew the Gospel message, but they did not all comprehend the good news. I continue to pray not just for opportunities to witness but for the ground to be made fertile for each chance to witness.

Pray for the Lord to move mightily in the hearts of your students; they cannot come to saving faith on their own.

Week 6 Day 3
Effectiveness and Opposition

Because a great door for effective work has opened to me, and there are many who oppose me.
1 Corinthians 16:9 (NIV)

In this chapter, Paul is describing the many physical and spiritual challenges that are mounting against him. While our work isn't technically the same as Paul's, we are still advancing the Gospel, which always attracts opposition. While teaching, we pour into countless students for 180 days of the year. Beyond education, there is a spiritual dimension to your classroom. This really is a "great door for effective work."

By the power of Christ, you are an effective ambassador for the Gospel and a threat to the enemy. Reflect on the reality of spiritual warfare that we often trivialize or dismiss. Remember that you have an enemy who is opposed to you. Satan knows that students in your class don't know Christ and will see Him in you. Your influence is so significant that Satan would love nothing more than to topple your career, marriage, and influence once and for all. Therefore, you need to make sure that you have a group of believers who commit to pray for you. This could be family, friends, or your church family. It could be all of the above; just reach out for committed prayer warriors to intervene on your behalf. Each day you are engaged in a battle; don't go in alone.

Be mindful of your opposition and recognize the great opportunity and blessing you have of being a teacher. There is a door that has been opened for you; proclaim Christ boldly!

Week 7 Day 1
Not 'Lording Over' Students

Be shepherds of God's flock that is under your care, watching over them—not because you must, but because you are willing, as God wants you to be; not pursuing dishonest gain, but eager to serve; not lording it over those entrusted to you, but being examples to the flock. And when the Chief Shepherd appears, you will receive the crown of glory that will never fade away.
1 Peter 5:2-5 (NIV)

As a first-year teacher, I was also a first-year coach, and I struggled with my authority. I would sometimes use my position to lord over students. I did this both as a teacher and as a coach. When I thought a student wasn't respecting me in the classroom, I would assert my authority over them. I had a senior girl in my psychology class one day who would not stop talking. I kept trying to lecture, and she kept distracting others. I finally called her out and said, "Don't you know that I control your grade? You should listen to me and show me more respect." She immediately stopped talking, but I could feel the sin in my heart, and the class's atmosphere shifted into uneasiness.

Around that time, I was on the court with the basketball team, helping out with the varsity team. Some of my athletes were whispering to each other and didn't get quiet as soon as I'd have liked. I told them to stop, and they did. The whole team looked at me; I felt vulnerable. I shouted for the entire team to start running laps in the gym until they "learned to respect me more." As they ran, I repeatedly told them that I could make them run all day, and I'd tell the head coach who to play next game.

Looking back on these examples, I see that this was just my insecurity dictating my behavior. I wasn't confident in my authority and sought to exercise it over students in a detrimental way. We are not supposed to talk to those under our authority that way. We are to be examples to our students and not oppress them by continually reminding them of our authority over them. No one wants to be around, much less in a classroom with, someone who always reminds them of the power dynamic between them. How would you feel if your principal greeted you, and everyone, by reminding you that they could fire you at any time? Students respond the same way when we continually tell them, "I can lower your grade," or, "I can make your day terrible in detention." Our position of authority is God-given and does not need to be verbalized every day. Instead, be an example to your students. We should exude confidence in our authority, knowing that it is God-given, God-enabled, and God-sustained.

We need to wield authority with humility and grace and do not need to weaponize our position over students.

Week 7 Day 2
Bound

I am obligated both to Greeks and non-Greeks, both to the wise and the foolish.
Romans 1:14 (NIV)

We cannot unfairly apply our time and our affection toward our students. Every student must be equally loved and cared for. I struggle with giving more attention to the good students or the ones whom I can hold a conversation with easily. I think of students at my international school who have more of a Western culture bent. They watch American movies and keep up to date with current events. It's easy for me to start a conversation with them. I even gravitate toward those conversations as a way to combat homesickness. I then find myself engaging them more consistently, often to the neglect of other students. This is favoritism and is counter to the life of a Christian. Not only are we professionally obligated to teach everyone, but we are spiritually as well. Remember that God specifically chooses the ordinary person to do mighty things through them. So, just as Paul was compelled to preach to all peoples, we are called to teach and love all our students.

Paul also preached to people of various intellectual abilities. He did not only teach to the learned but the uneducated as well. We are also in the classroom to serve all of our students. You are there to help all students achieve. That outgoing "A" student needs you, but also that reserved "C+" student is desperate for your guidance.

Ethnicity and test scores may divide our students, but what unites them is our commitment to them. Don't play favorites, and be sure to teach every student each day.

Week 7 Day 3
Actively Pursue Good

Do not withhold good from those to whom it is due, / when it is in your power to act.
Proverbs 3:27 (NIV)

The daily responsibilities we face are overwhelming. Between the lesson planning, professional development, and discipline follow-up, the last thing we have time for is praise. Apart from a positive comment on a paper, students rarely receive adequate feedback when doing something right.

These moments of praise can be academic or behavioral. Two stories come to my mind. The first was a student struggling with writing the AP style of essay questions in US History. This student wrote essay after essay and couldn't crack above a B- on the rubric. She came in for tutoring, studied hard, and still struggled for most of the school year. Then one day, she wrote an essay in class that was phenomenal. She did everything on the rubric and earned an A+. I was so excited for her. I wrote comments on the paper but felt compelled to write her an email as well. I praised her for her hard work, her argument, and the brilliant evidence that she utilized. I ended the email by telling her that I was now confident she would do very well on the AP exam, and she should be too. She responded with just a "Thanks!" so I thought I had just wasted my time affirming her.

It wasn't until the next year when she asked for a letter of recommendation for college that she opened up. She explained how she had been at her lowest point. She thought her writing was getting worse and was thinking about not even taking the exam. My email had lifted her spirits more than she could describe. I was totally shocked and humbled. I had no idea the Lord would use me to part the clouds of depression for one of my students.

I also remember another precious moment of affirmation for another student one year. In my class, I had the pleasure of teaching a student with severe learning disabilities and a hearing impairment. I do lots of group work in my class, so I was always careful to place the student in the best learning environment. This proved to be a challenge, especially if I needed to arrange groups on the fly. But early in the year, I had another student who was also a believer. This student voluntarily left their friends to partner up with my student with special needs. They consistently made an effort to help, mentor, and shepherd this student. I was so moved and proud of this student, especially since they were a believer. For most of the year, I just assumed that this sacrificial student knew my appreciation for them, but I never mentioned it.

Finally, an opportunity came, and I was eager to take advantage. I didn't know what exactly to say, but I knew I wanted to recognize their faith and the evident love of Christ in their life. I had a great mini-speech prepared but could only get out a few sentences; I was too overcome with emotion. I just told the student that I appreciated them loving my special needs student so well and that they were making the Lord proud. I said their faith was evident and encouraged them to continue to love as Christ loves us. I had to look away, as tears were welling in my eyes. I don't know what impact that affirmation had, but I pray that the Lord uses it powerfully. I know for me, the Lord has used others' words to affirm, comfort, challenge, and encourage me. As a result, my faith has been made stronger.

Scripture is clear that we need to be obedient and do good to our students when it is within our power. We are teachers and mentors to these students, and our words have incredible power. What if He will use that acknowledgment to transform the trajectory of their life? We need to go out of our comfort zone and speak life into and over our students. These moments don't need to be grand or eloquent either. Perhaps you could simply notify a parent when their student does something incredible. Or write a small note on a test or shoot off an email. A quick affirmation could have an immeasurable impact on a student's life.

We discipline consistently; let us not forget to also praise with equal enthusiasm.

Week 8 Day 1
Covert Christianity

You are the light of the world. A city situated on a hill cannot be hidden. No one lights a lamp and puts it under a basket, but rather on a lampstand, and it gives light for all who are in the house.
Matthew 5:14-15 (ESV)

As a teacher in a public school, I always struggled with just how much I could say and not break the law or violate the separation of church and state. However, the Lord revealed to me that I was overthinking the entire issue. I don't need to try to reword Scripture or speak in code. Sometimes the best way to communicate the Gospel is to explain a biblical perspective without quoting the Bible. This may sound complicated, but it is surprisingly easy.

The following conversation is an example of this approach and occurred during my third year of teaching.

Student: "Coach Way, yes or no, once you get married, you can still go to the strip club."

Me: (in my head) Wow! What do I say to that? I had never been asked that before. Strip club? Should I reprimand them for even asking me that?

Well, I thought, at least this group of students was asking me an honest question and trusted me to give them an honest answer. That does say something about our relationship. I decided to address the issue but provide a biblical answer embedded in my opinion.

I responded, "No to both. I don't believe it is right to go to a strip club before or after marriage. I think it is degrading to women, and strip clubs are terrible things to go to."

Student: (with a look of disbelief) "What?! That's crazy. So, let me get this straight you have never been to and will never go to a strip club?"

Me: (with the same amount of disbelief at their answer as they had at mine) "That is correct. A real man doesn't go to strip clubs but respects women and loves only his wife for life."

The whole group started laughing. They couldn't believe I said something so crazy.

Several guys shook their heads and just said, "Well, that's you but not me!"

This was not the ending to the conversation I was expecting. And at first, I was disappointed that I hadn't converted them.

As they returned to their conversation, I realized that if I didn't convince them to change their morality and worldview, it was okay. It wasn't my job at that moment to rain down fire and provide an altar call. However, I did expose them to a different look at life, a perspective they might not have heard before. Even though I didn't quote the Bible, I explained what God says about lust, marriage, and monogamy. In the end, that's all I can do. That's all God called for me to speak at that moment in time. I know that I was obedient, and hopefully, a seed was planted. Who knows how God might use that interaction in the future? That is not for me to stress about or micromanage. We are just called to be witnesses when He provides an opportunity.

You are a light on a hill, you cannot be hidden. Don't overthink your witness. God made you to shine so that all will see. No pressure to be a hero; do what you are called to do. God will take care of the rest.

Week 8 Day 2
Keep Your Decrees Part 1

It is not for kings to drink wine, not for rulers to crave beer, lest they drink and forget what has been decreed, and deprive all the oppressed of their rights.
Proverbs 31:4b-5 (NIV)

This verse demonstrates the power and consequences of a king's decision and the dangers of changing your mind on significant issues. You may not have been born into royalty, but I believe every teacher has a fief (their classroom), and we make countless decisions a day, many of which have significant consequences. What we say goes for our students every day. So, if you make a rule, keep it. If phones are not allowed in your classroom, then they are not allowed. You can't make one rule on Monday and go back on it by Wednesday. It is easy to cave some days, but you cannot capitulate.

I learned this lesson all too well. One semester I decided to use positive reinforcement to cure the "not doing homework disease." I decided to give students a ticket for high quiz grades or completed homework. They could use these tickets to get extra credit or save them all to "buy" some snacks at the end of the year. This strategy worked for a time. Homework was turned in more frequently, and grades improved; I was happy. However, I soon became behind and overwhelmed with all my grading. I didn't have the time to give out tickets and wanted to pass out work quickly. One day, I dropped weeks' worth of work when the bell rang without tickets attached, hoping students wouldn't notice.

I didn't even make it around the room before I heard, "So . . . we aren't getting tickets now?"

Embarrassed that I had been called out, I tried to save face. I said, "Well, not on this assignment."

I looked around the room and saw the disappointed faces of students who had worked hard and earned a higher grade but did not get the ticket that I had promised. I had just unilaterally changed the rules. I had broken my word with them. Such a small decision destroyed my rapport with students.

As a result of this one decision, I lost authority; my students lost trust in me. It was harder to teach because I had created a classroom environment that was not based on stability. Each time I said their homework was due, would my kids believe me? This was a catastrophic blow to my class morale. I had to rebuild relationships for weeks to continue to lead my students.

Most importantly, this lie harmed my witness. I was acting in a way that Jesus does not. I let my stress and laziness stop me from following through on my procedures. Our Father is a God of making and keeping promises. He cannot lie, and He always keeps His word. We must model the stability and faithfulness of God to our students.

Honor your commitments. If you make a decree, keep it.

Week 8 Day 3
Keep Your Decrees Part 2
It is not for kings to drink wine, not for rulers to crave beer, lest they drink and forget what has been decreed, and deprive all the oppressed of their rights.
Proverbs 31:4b-5 (NIV)

I want to look at the second half of the verses we read yesterday. In my first year of teaching, I learned a powerful lesson about depriving the oppressed of their rights. This story is hard for me to tell, but I want the experience to be conveyed so that you don't make the same mistake I did.

I had a student in my class who was medically hard of hearing and needed to be seated in the front of the class. One day I could not keep my class focused and quiet. I am embarrassed to admit it, but it was not a textbook classroom management day for me. I felt like I was moments away from a coup; I could not get control of my classroom.

I walked to one side of the room to stop a fight, and then a cell phone came out on the other side. When I ran over there to collect it, an argument began between two girls in the back row. You get the idea. I was so frustrated that I stopped trying to discipline, and I decided to talk over everything. I didn't try to teach well but just plowed through the lesson. It was a noise tug-of-war. Students started laughing, so I lectured louder. There was a lull, so I started talking faster. Back and forth and back and forth—it was exhausting.

After the lesson, I felt relieved and proud that I finished the lecture.

Wow, great job getting through that with all of that going against you," I told myself.

When the bell rang, my hearing-impaired student in the front row came up to me and said, "Coach Way, I enjoyed the lesson but couldn't hear or concentrate.

Now I'm worried about doing well on my quiz." He was sincere, and the look of anxiousness on his face made my stomach drop. I realized that I had neglected half of my students' learning by not being firm enough with the other half.

Because I had not managed my class well, my students were not taught. Learning did not occur. This is a terrible outcome for any student, but it is even worse for a student with special needs. He requires special care in a quiet classroom, and I deprived him of that. I couldn't believe I thought I taught a good lesson.

The Lord convicted me that I must stand up for all my students. They need an advocate in the classroom to protect and ensure their education. I need to teach every student and make sure they are all treated with love and care. I need to do all in my power to make sure that I don't deprive any student of the right to an education. Classroom management wasn't for me but for my students.

The real barometer of education is not finishing your

PowerPoint but standing up for those who need us the most.

Week 9 Day 1
Do All

For I have learned to be content whatever the circumstances. I know what it is to be in need, and I know what it is to have plenty. I have learned the secret of being content in any and every situation, whether well fed or hungry, whether living in plenty or in want. I can do all this through him who gives me strength.
Philippians 4:11-13 (NIV)

Philippians 4:13 is often misinterpreted to mean that there is nothing that you can't do with God as your strength. People will quote this before they run a marathon or do something else challenging. Although God does give us strength, and He can do anything, this verse means something much better. Let's paraphrase this verse and apply it to our school life.

Through it all, I know what it is like to have a "good" class and a difficult one. I have learned the secret of being content in any and every situation, whether a flawless lesson plan or one that utterly fails, whether appreciated or taken for granted, whether underpaid or overworked, whether having unforgettable students or students I try to forget, whether in career advancements or demotions. I can do all things through Him who gives me strength.

We do not let our circumstances define us or our teaching. We do not wallow in challenges. Even if we have the worst possible school year, we can endure all things because He is the source of our strength. There is nothing that comes across our path that Christ has not already given us the victory over. This victory does not mean we are given superhuman strength to win a weightlifting competition. We won't run a marathon, but we will win the race. We can remain content in the good and bad times, recognizing that Christ's death and power triumph over every one of our circumstances.

What incredible power our Savior possesses!

Week 9 Day 2
Cyclical Praise
The LORD is my strength and my shield; my heart trusts in him, and he helps me. My heart leaps for joy, and with my song, I praise him.
Psalm 28:7 (NIV)

I love this cycle that the Psalmist describes and have found it to be true.

The Lord is all-powerful and our defender. When we apply that truth to our life, it causes us to trust Him more. When we trust Him more, He reveals more of Himself to us. The more intimately we walk with Him, the more we realize His great love for us. His love compels our hearts to jump for joy out of appreciation and praise. We now see God as even stronger than before. We trust Him beyond what we thought possible. We then grow in intimacy where His grace is even sweeter than before, and the incredible cycle begins again.

We trust God. We love Him more. He then gives us more presence, which causes joy and results in praise. On and on. Each cycle is richer and more meaningful than before. Growing in faith is growing more in love for God.

Take time today to meditate on His love and power. Put more trust in Him both at school and in your personal life, and see that you will soon find joy, and you will praise the only One who is worthy.

Week 9 Day 3
Value in Christ Over GPA

For you know that it was not with perishable things such as silver or gold that you were redeemed from the empty way of life handed down to you from your ancestors, but with the precious blood of Christ, a lamb without blemish or defect.
1 Peter 1:18-19 (NIV)

One of the most impactful people in my Christian college experience was a math professor who prayed over us before every test. The practice of praying for a test was familiar to me; I've done it ever since I remember taking tests. In fact, my test-taking prayer life was strong. "God, please help me to get an A on this thing." But her prayer was much different than mine. She asked the Lord that the fruits of our studying would be evident on the test but that we would remember that our value came solely from God. She mentioned that because Jesus had given His life for us, it demonstrated that He valued us dearly. Therefore, our worth could not be derived from an algebra test because it was already infinitely greater.

Our Savior values us, which is infinitely more determinative of our worth than any test, GPA, profession, or other earthly thing. Our redemption, our right standing with God, was bought with Christ's blood. He demonstrates our value to Him by giving Himself up for us. And His blood is incorruptible; it won't go away. His love cannot fade, and our value to Him will never diminish.

Her test-taking prayer was so much better than mine and completely changed my perspective on test-taking. Tests were a time to show what I knew, but I was selling myself short when I used them to determine my value. The problem of putting my value in my grades worked both ways. If I did poorly, I could become depressed, while with an A+ I could be filled with pride—what a paradigm-shifting lesson to learn in a math class. Our value is rooted in Christ and not our achievements, and that's very good news.

I now have the privilege of praying this same prayer over my students before every test. I pray for them to see this test as only a test and not base their value on it. I ask God to put His love in their hearts so that they may know the security of His love. Working at a private school, I'm able to pray audibly. But when I worked in public school, I silently interceded for my students as I distributed tests.

In all circumstances, I trust the Lord is working on their hearts as He did on mine. Test scores are idols that assign us less value than what God says about us. Who knows when God will get hold of a heart and shake it free of idolatry?

Each test, I am reminded that my students and my worth are thankfully not tied to an assessment but bound to Christ Himself.

Will you pray for your students? Will you pray for yourself?

Week 10 Day 1
Sacrifice Comes Second

To do righteousness and justice is desired by the LORD more than sacrifice.
Proverbs 21:3 (NASB1995)

It is easy to self-martyrize our profession and ourselves. I find myself going about saying woe is me because I am a teacher. I make comments about poor pay or problems in the education system. I'm constantly tearing down the system just to show how benevolent I am to work at fixing it.

We sometimes disparage our situations to elevate our importance in the minds of ourselves and those we encounter. We want to elaborate on our struggle to accentuate our sacrifice. But even though you are sacrificing a lot of your time and energy as a teacher, sacrifice isn't what's most important to the Lord. God cares much more about your daily habits of righteousness and justice than your sacrifice. If you neglect Him but pour yourself out for your students, He doesn't honor that sacrifice. God is not impressed by your late nights. Each time you pay for your own supplies with an unloving heart does not make you holier.

How you grow closer to God and love your students mean more to Him than people thinking you're a great person because you are a teacher.

If we idolize the sacrifice of teaching, we miss out on what's most important to God.

Week 10 Day 2
God Has Won the Battle
Then Deborah said to Barak, "Go! This is the day the LORD has given Sisera into your hands. Has not the LORD gone ahead of you?"
Judges 4:14 (NIV)

Before my first day teaching in a new school overseas, I was overwhelmed with stress and doubt. Uncertainties about fitting in with staff and connecting with students from cultures that I had never taught before pushed me into fear. Despite praying for this school year for months, my unbelief still prevailed. Then the Lord rebuked me with this verse from Judges. He had called me overseas, which meant that all my fear was unfounded.

The upcoming school year, with all its unknowns, had already been won by the Lord. He had already gone ahead of me, answered my prayers, and achieved the victory. While I was stressing, He had already orchestrated every detail of my new job for my good and His glory. I repented of my unbelief and took hold of His faithfulness.

Maybe you are feeling similar stresses and fears about an unknown this school year. Like myself and Barak, I encourage you, "Go! This is the school year the Lord has given you!"

Week 10 Day 3
Enjoying Parent Conferences

In the same way, let your light shine before others, that they may see your good deeds and glorify your Father in heaven.
Matthew 5:16 (NIV)

In my years as a teacher, I have not always had a great attitude about parent-teacher conferences. They are never at a convenient time, and they usually arise because of some existing conflict. No matter how hard I try, I can't help but go into each conference on the defensive, ready to pull out all the evidence to prove my point. Sadly, I approached conferences this way for years. I was so focused on myself that I never saw the "bigger picture" about what a conference is and what it could be.

All of this changed during one conference in late spring. I was meeting with a mom of a student who was turning in his papers so late that it was pulling his average dangerously low. I came in with the usual lousy attitude, ready to defend my late policy and tell this mom that this situation was all her son's fault. It is interesting how easily our sin nature rears its wicked head when we feel like our pride is being challenged. As the meeting began, she asked several questions, and I answered them. Surprisingly, after a few minutes, she was on my side and apologized for her son's behavior. She said she would check with him every day until he turned in his work. She also promised that it would never happen again. I was stunned; the meeting was over before it began.

However, she didn't get up and walk out; instead, she leaned forward with pain in her eyes. She looked at me and asked a question I will never forget, "Does my son have friends?" I was so shocked by the question and the vulnerability that I couldn't think of what to say for ten seconds. All of a sudden, the purpose of this meeting manifested itself in my mind. She was not concerned as much about her son's grade as about his well-being at school. She was not looking for a fight but some encouragement and hope. I felt so petty and selfish. I was so concerned about my pride that I didn't consider that this meeting could be about anything else.

I told her that he had several friends and was popular in school. He was funny and enjoyed by all members of his grade. I also affirmed that he was a diligent worker in another class I taught him in. Her demeanor changed as these reassurances washed over her. Toward the end of the conversation, she broke down and wept. She lamented that he doesn't talk with her as much anymore and that she worried that he didn't have friends at school. She was so glad to know that all her fears had been unfounded. She left with a smile on her face and encouragement in her heart.

I, on the other hand, was so humbled. Here I was, preoccupied with my little world, and right in front of me, a mom wanted to see if her son was okay.

Wow. How unimportant my late policy felt.

This was a significant moment of clarity for me, and I

learned two main things that I try to take into every parent-teacher conference. The first lesson was that God has planned every parent-teacher conference for a purpose. The timing may be inconvenient for you, but it is never random. Each conference is a divine appointment, so don't lament them. Ask Him for the grace to see the conference with His plan in mind.

The second lesson is that we should never let our teacher duties overshadow our role to shepherd our students. At the end of the day, students are still kids. They need love, support, and advocates. We have to remember that God has given them to us to educate but also to care for. They aren't just names in our grade books. They need us. Their parents need our help as well. We should strive not to be antagonistic toward parents but partner with them in their children's care. We should rejoice in every opportunity to let our light shine.

Do your best to see the value of and anticipate the great things that can come from every parent-teacher conference.

Week 11 Day 1
Recipients of Grace

But when the goodness and loving kindness of God our Savior appeared, he saved us, not because of works done by us in righteousness, but according to his own mercy, by the washing of regeneration and renewal of the Holy Spirit, whom he poured out on us richly through Jesus Christ our Savior, so that being justified by his grace we might become heirs according to the hope of eternal life.
Titus 3:4-7 (ESV)

I love this detailed explanation of the Gospel. As a teacher, wielding authority and respect, I am prone to pride. I see classroom success as a result of my careful planning. If I'm not careful, this elevated view of myself can distort my understanding of the Gospel. I begin to think that maybe God saved me because I was already pretty good, but He wants to make me better. Or, perhaps, I was just better than other people, and that's why I was saved.

Lest we become arrogant and boast, we are reminded in these verses that we did not earn salvation. It was because of His goodness and loving kindness that He saved us. We did not do righteous works to merit salvation, but it is only because of His mercy that we were saved. After receiving this mercy, we also didn't begin to make ourselves better. It was God the Holy Spirit who regenerated and renewed us. And if that wasn't incredible enough, Christ then generously poured out the Holy Spirit on us so that we might become heirs and have hope in eternal life.

What an incredible reality our conversion experience

was! May the truth of the Gospel continually renew our minds and refresh our hearts.

Pray that this news shapes your actions and motivates your love today.

Week 11 Day 2

Created for Good Works

For we are God's handiwork, created in Christ Jesus to do good works, which God prepared in advance for us to do.
Ephesians 2:10 (NIV)

Our whole purpose in this life is to do good works so that people will see them and give God all the glory. It is exciting to realize that every day, every period God has, before time began, placed opportunities in our paths in which we can glorify Him. What an incredible truth.

We were made for Him with a purpose. Each day He has given us something meaningful to do. We get to show the love of our Father to bring Him glory. There is purpose in every day. Once I realized this truth, I began praying for the wisdom to recognize these opportunities and to act on them. These good works come in many forms. They come in your lesson plans and in teaching well but are not limited to your job. We need to be aware that there will be a time before class or afterward to accomplish the good work God has laid out for us to do.

One thing I struggle with is being so uptight about keeping the academic pace that when an opportunity arises, I neglect it for "time's sake." I remember a particularly persistent student who would not let me alone to start class. I begrudgingly listened to him, but the whole time I kept thinking about how if class started late, I wouldn't get everything covered that I needed to. He then asked me a profound and spiritually-related question. Thankfully, I was able to offer him some encouragement, and he quickly took his seat.

I realized afterward that God planned that conversation. I was made to offer that encouragement in hopes that he will see that good work and glorify God. I was so focused on my job that I almost missed my calling.

We are to be excellent teachers, but don't be so narrow-minded about keeping a schedule that you miss out on the good works you were made for. Ask the Lord for spiritual eyes to see what He has in store for you today.

Week 11 Day 3
Asking for Advice is a Necessity

For lack of guidance a nation falls, / but victory is won through many advisers.
Proverbs 11:14 (NIV)

Caring mentors significantly shaped me in my early years. I would not be the teacher I am today without them. Scripture affirms this by saying that victory is made possible through many advisors. Regardless of how many years you have been teaching, you need wise people around you.

In every stage of our careers, we need a seasoned hand to guide us in the uncertain waters of education. We all need people to help ride out the storm and avoid the jagged rocks on the edge.

I cannot stress enough the crucial importance of finding mentors and people who will pour into your life. I would suggest at least two teachers (either in your school or in the district) and one spiritual mentor who can challenge you apart from educational responsibilities. I did not initially seek this arrangement, but God provided these people for me.

I have found that a group of advisors gives you objectivity and perspectives from which you can discern wisdom. It would help if you ran significant decisions regarding your career, particular struggles, and possible solutions by your trusted support system.

Arrogance and a lack of advisors will bring your classroom to ruin. Because of the unique stress of our positions, we need advice from others that care about us. No teacher is an island. Ask the Lord to bring mentors into your life and joyfully surround yourself with wise counsel.

Week 12 Day 1
Don't Work in Vain
Unless the LORD builds the house, the builders labor in vain. Unless the LORD watches over the city, the guards stand watch in vain.
Psalm 127:1 (NIV)

Whether you are a veteran or a new teacher, success is dependent on how much we allow the Lord to plan and build our classroom. In my first year of teaching, it was easy to call out to the Lord in desperation for Him to move because everything about the job was unknown. However, the longer I teach, the harder this becomes. The more I've taught the same subject or worked in the same school, the more I start to attribute student progress and data-driven improvement to me and the lessons I've built. But this attitude is unbiblical. When we see the fruit of our labor as the result of only ourselves, we are in dangerous territory. In fact, I could be less effective the more experience I have if I lean more on my own ability and less on the Lord's.

We need Scripture to humble us and right our thinking. I think about this verse and what it's communicating about our efforts and God's power. Builders would physically build a house but not consult the Lord. Likewise, a guard watches over the town all night, hoping to protect it from attack. However, because the Lord is not in the work, the work is in vain. In both of these examples, the individual trusts their effort and their work to accomplish what they want.

The builder is relying on his skill to create a house that will last a long time. The guard is trusting his ability to keep the city safe. He thinks that he can protect his loved ones. But Scripture says that his effort, and ours, is entirely insufficient to accomplish what we want. It doesn't say the Lord and the builder build the house, or that the Lord and the guard both watch over the city. Instead, it says the Lord makes the house. The Lord watches over the town. He is the only one who can build a durable house and keep a city safe. You could put an army of a million men to protect a town, but without the Lord, they can't repel any attack.

As the Psalmist says, if we don't invite the Lord to work, our efforts are in vain. If we want to be the most effective teacher and to have the positive impact we desire, the Lord and the Lord alone has to build that foundation and affect that change.

Are you trusting in your own abilities?

Do you really think that you are powerful enough to achieve what you want?

Are you working tirelessly designing lessons and grading papers but neglecting the Lord?

Do you have plans for your classrooms that you have not consulted Him on or asked His help in actuating?

If we don't daily ask the Lord to move in our lessons, the lessons and all our work behind them will have been in vain.

Week 12 Day 2
Seeking Only the Glory of Christ

Whoever speaks on their own does so to gain personal glory, but he who seeks the glory of the one who sent him is a man of truth; there is nothing false about him.
John 7:18 (NIV)

The temptation of pride is never far from us. In the course of a typical school day, there are several opportunities to elevate yourself. These temptations are subtle and seemingly harmless. However, if not spiritually discerned and appropriately answered, you could be building an altar to yourself without even realizing it.

Here are some examples of times when I've easily succumbed to pride.

I was at the copier, and I was asked how my kids did on the most recent test compared to the other history teacher.

A new teacher asked how I manage my classroom so effectively.

A former student showed up, thanking me for teaching them and changing their life.

How is a Christian to react to so many different scenarios that just beg for you to pat yourself on the back?

Without humility and the Holy Spirit's conviction, such praise can easily lead us down the path of sin. I have learned to respond with sincerity and quickly affirm others in my life who have made the compliment possible. This helps redirect the conversation and lets the other person know that you don't see yourself as the only influence on the situation.

Now, for my own heart in those times, I look to this verse to remind me to seek God's glory and not my own. I'm not out to teach so that I am remembered. I'm not about building my kingdom but my Father's. Part of that humility comes from recognizing the truth that we are utterly incapable of doing anything apart from Him. As Scriptures says here, the humble man is described as truthful because he points to God's glory. If you preach your own glory, you rob the glory that God is owed. The man who glorifies God and not himself is honest. He fully knows Who is sovereign and good.

Don't lie and speak of your glory but only of His.

Week 12 Day 3
Judged More Harshly

Not many of you should become teachers, my fellow believers, because you know that we who teach will be judged more strictly. We all stumble in many ways. Anyone who is never at fault in what they say is perfect, able to keep their whole body in check.
James 3:1-2 (NIV)

This verse continually terrifies and humbles me. While I believe that this verse's original context applies to teachers of the Word, the exhortation is also for us. Because of our enormous influence on thousands of people throughout our lifetime, we are just as liable for our speech and conduct. Our lives are on full display to students for 180 days of the year.

I'm sure you remember your favorite teacher or professor growing up. I became a teacher partly because of key teachers in my life. Truly the influence of a teacher is tremendous. With significant impact comes great responsibility. Our words and actions can build or destroy. Inspire or decimate. Our habits, the jokes we tell, how we treat each student will be remembered for a lifetime in our students' hearts and minds.

We don't have to be perfect, but we do need to keep our whole body in check. Is our thought life under control in the classroom? Are we mindful of our students each day? Are we seeking the Lord's leading in ministering to their needs? Are we fighting the sin in our own lives? What we say and do matters. And even after the school year, we may stay in contact with students for many years after graduation. We have the unique privilege of shepherding a soul. God doesn't take this lightly, and neither should we. We will be judged more strictly than non-teachers according to how we influenced our students. We will be held accountable for our witness, and so we should step into our classrooms each day with humility and in His power. This reality should motivate and drive us to daily prayer.

O, Lord, please help us to walk in Your ways. Please help us to model You to our students. Keep our thoughts, words, and deeds in submission to You. May You be glorified in our example. Thank You for the incredible privilege of being a part of Your kingdom's advancement in our classrooms. Please help us to honor You in all we do. Amen.

Week 13 Day 1
Victory Despite Failure

My flesh and my heart may fail, / but God is the strength of my heart and my portion forever.
Psalm 73:26 (ESV)

Failure is difficult for everyone, but especially for teachers. We are the only adult in the classroom. We need to be the expert and the one who has it all together. But teaching is an incredibly taxing ministry that requires abundant physical energy and constant care toward our students. Despite our best wishes, we fail in these areas. Some days we lack the energy to teach as we should. Some days our heart isn't in it, and we go through the motions. Tragically, sometimes we are so burned out that we teach with apathy rather than zeal.

However, in our failure, God brings salvation. In this area, He is opposite to us in every way. We may fail; He never will. Our strength will fade. He is limitless. Our passion wanes, and His remains. Our affections to Him are fickle while His love and commitment to us are everlasting. We can take comfort, then, that when we fail, God provides all that we need. His perfection covers our inadequacies.

Find in Him your all-in-all today, and be reassured that He is your portion this school year and forever.

Week 13, Day 2
Living Out the Power of His Promise

Now the eleven disciples went to Galilee, to the mountain to which Jesus had directed them. And when they saw him they worshiped him, but some doubted. And Jesus came and said to them, "All authority in heaven and on earth has been given to me. Go therefore and make disciples of all nations, baptizing them in the name of the Father and of the Son and of the Holy Spirit, teaching them to observe all that I have commanded you. And behold, I am with you always, to the end of the age."
Matthew 28:16-20 (ESV)

Two truths stand out as encouragement in the Great Commission. Firstly, Jesus says that "all authority in heaven and earth has been given" to Him. If we don't read carefully, we can easily miss this incredible statement. No longer is Jesus masking His power on earth, but he is now asserting His just and sovereign authority over the earth. I love the totality of this truth. All authority has been given to Him—not some or most, all. Do you speak to Christ as One with all authority? And even if you believe that He has the authority to help in your problems, do you also believe that He has the authority to rule over you? Do you submit to Jesus as your rightful master?

Secondly, after commanding that we are all to make disciples from all nations, Jesus tells us that He is with us and will never leave us. This is not just sentimental; Jesus is stating the reality of the new covenant. He promises not to leave us as we do all that He has commanded. When we teach, we are not alone. When you are in over your head, remember that He is with you. There will never be a time in your life or eternity that you will ever be alone. Jesus is with you now and forever.

We connect these ideas to reveal a truth that should give us confidence and a grateful heart.

The task of making disciples around the world is enormous, seemingly impossible. Despite this, we are still commanded to do so. How can we complete such a task? We can't. On our own, we would fail. However, we are not alone. We are called and equipped to spread the Gospel by Christ Himself. Christ has been given all authority, and He will help us accomplish His will. He does not call us to do something in which we must prove our worth to Him. He is there to help us with all of the power and the might of the universe. We are His ambassadors on His mission, acting with His authority. We should evangelize and disciple with the assurance that we are in the Lord's will and have the Lord with us. This is what it looks like to live in the power of the promise. To take Jesus at His word and trust His power and fellowship always to guide us as we have the privilege of seeing His kingdom advance.

Stand tall in your classroom. Take pleasure in serving King Jesus, for He is with you, and with Him, all things are possible. However, because the Lord is not in the work, the work is in vain. In both of these examples, the individual trusts their effort and their work to accomplish what they want.

Week 13 Day 3
Giving Credit Where Credit is Due

The horse is made ready for the day of battle, / but the victory belongs to the LORD.
Proverbs 21:31 (ESV)

The horse being made ready for battle means that there are specific actions that are taken in order to win a battle. A king couldn't just run out and face his enemy without proper preparations. Apart from his army, a king would need to shoe his horse, train him for battle, and make sure he was well fed and rested.

I think of my classroom as the battle and my lesson plan, prayer, classroom management, and relationships with students as the horse—the better the preparation, the higher our chances of success. We are responsible for preparing well for each day. Not having any classroom materials ready is not living by faith but being unfaithful to our responsibilities. As Christians, we are called to do our jobs with excellence and work for God and His glory. Once these preparations are made, God then invites us to fight alongside Him in our classrooms. We get the privilege of fighting together with the God of the universe; how incredible!

The last part of the verse then conveys a humbling and encouraging truth: "but the victory belongs to the Lord." With all our meticulous preparation and hard work, it can be easy to pat ourselves on the back after a great day and take credit for the magic that happened in our rooms. I remember sometimes playing back moments in class that I was particularly proud of and thinking that only a great teacher like me could have done that. Then the Lord lovingly reminded me of this verse. Although God allows us to go to battle with Him, we cannot claim the victory. It wasn't our preparation or careful planning that made our classes run smoothly. We didn't orchestrate that moment to love students. You are a participant but not the deciding factor. Victory belongs to God alone. God doesn't cause most victories or some victories but every victory. I am victorious but not the victor.

To further expand this point, consider if God wasn't with you. What if you prepared your lessons, and God sought to fight against you? Would you still achieve victory? Could even one of your desires happen without Him? If we can't win without Him, how can we believe we cause success with Him?

If you win the battle, the credit belongs to God alone. Continue to prepare and to fight, but remember Who deserves the glory.

Week 14 Day 1
Defend the Weak

Speak up for those who cannot speak for themselves, for the rights of all who are destitute. Speak up and judge fairly; defend the rights of the poor and needy.
Proverbs 31:8-9 (NIV)

I don't know if you ever eavesdrop as you walk the halls, but every time I do, my heart breaks for students. The vulgarity and degradation students inflict on each other is appalling. This is not just bullying but a daily and continual barrage of insults, ridicule, and harassment. No one is safe from being maligned. The students who suffer the most are those who are at the bottom of the social ladder. They are the most vulnerable, the least able to defend themselves. Therefore, it is our responsibility as Christians and as teachers to follow Scripture and protect those who can't speak for themselves.

In my first year of teaching, this happened in my class. I had a student with a learning disability in class, and he was a delight to teach. He was respectful and always had a smile on his face. One day another student began calling him names and mocking the way he talked. I couldn't believe what I was hearing. Righteous indignation built up in me, and I immediately called the student out in the hall. I didn't even wait for the door to close before I tore into him. I lectured him up and down, making sure to convey how unacceptable that behavior was in my classroom.

He was very remorseful. He apologized and never mocked the other student in my classroom again.

I think there is sometimes hesitancy with Christians to call out unbiblical behavior. We may try to be more diplomatic and might see my reaction in this story as going too far. But I disagree. The swiftness of action correlates to the severity of the issue. Whenever there is clear discrimination and your students' rights are being violated, you must act swiftly. This is not the time for a listening exercise between you and the guilty student. You have God-given and God-ordained authority. You are in that classroom and with those students to exercise that authority as God has said you are. If you neglect this duty, then you are not teaching according to God's Word but according to your preferences. God has commanded you to stand up for the weak, so you must do it. You have to make it absolutely clear that that behavior is not tolerated even one iota in your classroom. A firm and direct denunciation of bullying is non-negotiable.

In doing this, not only will you defend those in your classroom who can't protect themselves, but you will show our Father's heart toward the lowly and oppressed.

Obey the Lord by defending the weak and protecting the vulnerable that He has given you.

Week 14 Day 2
Pray to Thrive, Not Survive
I have fought the good fight, I have finished the race, I have kept the faith.
2 Timothy 4:7 (ESV)

Paul's perseverance and faithful ministry are inspiring. He penned these words to Timothy as he reflected on his life. Paul never stopped serving the Lord, even to his martyrdom. Paul had a clear vision of finishing well. He never settled for just getting by. In all situations, he continually decided to persevere. We can learn a lot from his example.

Regardless of our situation, we need to pray to thrive, not just survive. Don't get me wrong, I have prayed, "Lord, please . . . just let me get through this week," several times. But creating a habit of cyclical "survival prayers" produces ministry short-sightedness. Only working for the next break disengages us from our purpose. If we always have our head down at the grindstone, we will also likely miss out on a divine appointment right in front of our noses. I can't tell you how many times I have let the minute stresses of the day steal my time. I'll focus on those things instead of loving students; I will be short with them and not intentionally connect so that I can focus more on myself and my perceived crises.

But, no matter the circumstances, no matter how terrible the day, God is still sovereign, and He has placed you in your classroom for a purpose. God has interwoven ministry opportunities within each period, each day, and each week.

We are called to finish the race. We need to keep our eyes fixed on the finish line, and with His strength, we will end well. Pray to run well each day and run to win the prize, not only to make it to the weekend.

Week 14 Day 3
Use Your Gift

Unless the LORD *builds the house, the builders labor in vain. Unless the* LORD *watches over the city, the guards stand watch in vain.*
Psalm 127:1 (NIV)

Whether you are a veteran or a new teacher, success is dependent on how much we allow the Lord to plan and build our classroom. In my first year of teaching, it was easy to call out to the Lord in desperation for Him to move because everything about the job was unknown. However, the longer I teach, the harder this becomes. The more I've taught the same subject or worked in the same school, the more I start to attribute student progress and data-driven improvement to me and the lessons I've built. But this attitude is unbiblical. When we see the fruit of our labor as the result of only ourselves, we are in dangerous territory. In fact, I could be less effective the more experience I have if I lean more on my own ability and less on the Lord's.

We need Scripture to humble us and right our thinking. I think about this verse and what it's communicating about our efforts and God's power. Builders would physically build a house but not consult the Lord. Likewise, a guard watches over the town all night, hoping to protect it from attack. However, because the Lord is not in the work, the work is in vain. In both of these examples, the individual trusts their effort and their work to accomplish what they want.

Week 15 Day 1
Teaching Unconditional Love
We love because he first loved us.
1 John 4:19 (ESV)

We are increasingly teaching students who have never heard of the Gospel. Consequently, they have never experienced or heard about unconditional love. When you do get the opportunity to explain unconditional love to a student, it is a transformative event.

I once had a student who didn't finish his homework and was copying down answers in the front row of the class. Long story short, I called him out on his action, which he began to deny. We went back and forth until I finally directed him to the hall, where we could continue the conversation. We went into the hall, and as soon as the door shut, he looked at me and said, "I've made you mad. I don't want you to be mad at me, Coach."

I was shocked. I thought he would continue arguing about what cheating was. Instead, he was more concerned about what his actions had done to our relationship. "I'm not mad at you," I said reassuringly. "I'm just frustrated that you cheated because I want you to be a better man, and you're selling yourself short."

He looked perplexed. "Okay, well, if you aren't mad, I bet you don't like me."

Before I answered, the Lord reminded me that I had said something similar to Him. I remember praying and saying, "Lord, even if I'm forgiven, you might love me less because of my sin." But that is not true. God loves us unconditionally. That means, He loves us, because He loves us. His love for you is rooted in His grace; it can't be earned or erased.

Now, every time my heart doubts His forgiveness I remind myself of this truth and He breathes His mercy and grace over me. He refreshes my soul with undeserved love.

I smiled and now understood what I had to explain to my student. I told him that my love for him was unconditional. My commitment to him would not change based on his behavior. That meant I would help him achieve his best and even apply to college regardless of how he treated me. I reminded him that the most important thing for me was to see him be successful. Even if he cussed me out every day, I was still going to love him.

His eyes and mouth were wide open.

He was in shock. He stood there, genuinely perplexed.

I invited him back to class, and he walked contemplatively back to his desk. He sat down and was quiet for the rest of the class. I think this was the first time someone ever explained the fantastic reality of unconditional love to him. He simply couldn't comprehend that he could be loved even when he was not loveable. This attribute of God is something I so often take for granted. God loved us when we were His enemies, and He adopted us as sons and daughters when there was nothing good in us. And after we have joined the family, He still loves us, even when we fail to love Him daily. That is life-changing news.

My heart smiled as I prayed that a seed was planted. I thanked God for His unconditional love toward me. I know that I am only able to love others because His heart-changing love enables me to. I cannot love without Him. He has so lavished us with His grace that it overflows and spills out onto others. What a privilege to replicate, even on a small scale, the love Jesus has toward me for this student.

Indeed, we love because He first loved us.

Week 15 Day 2
Be Mindful of Every Word
But I tell you that every careless word that people speak, they shall give an accounting for it in the day of judgment.
Matthew 12:36 (NASB1995)

This declaration by Jesus always convicts me. I think back to all of the passing conversations where I made fun of a new procedure or rule. How often I complained about every little thing.

I particularly remember all of the discussions during lunch in the teacher's lounge, and I shudder. How many days did I sit in there and gossip about teachers and coworkers? How easily did I slander and malign everyone I thought had negatively impacted me and my classroom? I am embarrassed that I will have to give account for every single one of those terrible things I said on the day of judgment. With those words, I not only damaged my integrity and witness but also disrupted intimacy with God.

Learn this lesson before I did and carefully guard every word that leaves your mouth, whether at school or home.

Week 15 Day 3
The Action of Love

Little children, let us not love with word or with tongue but in deed and in truth.
1 John 3:18 (ESV)

Love is not just an abstract concept. Love is always accompanied by action. We know God loves us not only because He says so but because Christ died for us. God proves His love for us through the act of Jesus' death, burial, and resurrection. Likewise, we demonstrate love to our students not just through words but with action.

I think one habit worth getting into as a teacher is being a servant. I believe we often miss small opportunities to be kind to our students. I know you are helpful to them, often more than they deserve. But what would it look like to love them sacrificially? What does going the extra mile look like in the classroom?

I saw another teacher do this very thing, and it challenged me to love my students better. The whole class was working in groups on an assignment. This teacher was monitoring the room when a student's pencil broke, and they didn't have another one. He asked if the teacher could get him a pencil from the pencil jar on her desk. To my amazement, she stopped what she was doing and got him a pencil. The student kept working, and she kept monitoring.

Inspired, I started to model this in my classroom. The first time I did this, I was amazed at the selfishness of my heart. I was walking around when a student asked me to sharpen their pencil after it broke. I was so resistant. Stand up and walk over there yourself, I thought. I'm busy walking around. But then this verse came to mind. The class was behaving well, and I had the time. What would it really cost me? What would the benefit be? Well, it would cost me all of thirty seconds of my time, but it would be a tangible example to show love to that student.

I decided to serve my student in this way. As I took the pencil and was sharpening it, I was surprised to see how good it was for me to die to my desires and show love to my kids. My heart was so cold and hardened, and this act of service softened me. I hadn't realized how accustomed I was to being served. In my position of authority, I so easily forget that true love is service. Even this small act is a way for that student to understand better the love I have for him. God willing, he will also see Jesus in this demonstration of love.

Now, we are not at our students' beck and call and most certainly should not enable them. I have seen kids take advantage of teachers, and that is certainly not loving. But I think many educators are so afraid to be taken advantage of that they don't practice service. Instead, they have justified the callousness surrounding their hearts. We are called to go the extra mile and to die to ourselves daily for the sake of the Gospel. The Holy Spirit helps us to know the difference between love and enablement. Ask Him for clarity, but commit yourself to serve your students. I challenge you to find new ways to show your students how much you care about them. Demonstrate your love to them and see their hearts, and yours, be transformed.

Week 16 Day 1
We Are Confined, but He is Not
For which I am suffering, bound with chains as a criminal. But the word of God is not bound!
2 Timothy 2:9 (ESV)

Teaching in a public school and wanting to share your faith explicitly can be like navigating a minefield. What does the wall of separation of church and state really mean? Can I say God? Can I reference Jesus but only as a historical figure? Can I be more open to a group of students than the whole class? You may start to say something to a student and then have to stop yourself for fear that quoting Scripture might be over the line.

Sometimes I would know exactly what advice to give a seeking student but feel like I couldn't. What if I lose my job by sharing my faith? What if I don't share my faith when God has called me to and thereby disobey Christ? Each day I felt as though my hands were tied, and I had to resort to vague methods of sharing my faith when I knew that a student needed to hear the truth clearly—not knowing where the line is can be frustrating. But chief among my concerns was wondering if I could be useful if I couldn't explicitly share Christ. Can the Gospel succeed with restrictions around it?

This verse answers that question in a resounding way. Paul is writing Timothy from prison, a much more restrictive place than my school. And by all accounts, it would seem that prison would stop the spread of the Gospel. How could people hear about Jesus if the

Lord's servant was in a jail cell? Paul answers this question with the confident declaration that although he is imprisoned, God is not! Even though Paul is confined, God cannot be confined.

We may feel our hands and our witness are bound, but man cannot bind God. No one can even slow Him or His work down. He will always accomplish His will and will always be victorious. No law is strong enough, and no wall of separation is high enough to restrict our Lord. No matter how clear or vague we are, the Spirit will move uninhibited. Therefore, we can witness with confidence knowing that God's kingdom will always advance.

I am comforted that my perception of restriction does not apply to God. Rejoice in His freedom and power to always triumph!

Week 16 Day 2
Tool in the Hand of the Master

Is the axe to boast itself over the one who chops with it? Is the saw to exalt itself over the one who wields it? . . . Therefore, the Lord, the GOD of hosts, will send a wasting disease among his stout warriors.
Isaiah 10:15-16 (NASB)

As I've previously mentioned, I am continually fighting against pride, and these verses in Isaiah always humble me. When I see success in my classroom, I start to think that it's all because of me.

But for me to take credit would be as ridiculous as an axe taking credit for cutting down a big tree or a saw thinking it caused a board to split. The saw and axe are just tools. If the axe or the saw were never picked up, they would be ineffective. They would be motionless tools lying on the ground, and the tree would remain standing. Even if an axe somehow picked itself up and flung itself against a tree, there is no way that tree is being cut down.

Similarly, my attempts to influence and teach will always amount to nothing if I am not wielded and used by the Master. For me to try to teach on my own is as futile as an axe lying in the grass. However, when God picks us up, He sharpens us and uses us to accomplish His purposes. It is not degrading to be a tool but our greatest joy. When we are tools in the hands of our Master, we get to experience His power as He works with and through us. We receive the benefit of also being a part of kingdom work. We get to marvel at His infinite wisdom as He accomplishes

His perfect will. We get to bask in His love, enjoying it like the warming sunshine on a dreary day. We think about all He has for us as we humbly serve Him out of gratitude.

All of these experiences are far and above what we could accomplish on our own. Through Him, we can see trees be chopped down that we could never have brought down independently. We are, therefore, elevated above our abilities and potential when He uses us.

What a blessing it is to be a tool in the hands of our loving Master.

Week 16 Day 3
Leading in the Storm

Since neither sun nor stars appeared for many days, and no small storm was assailing us, from then on all hope of our being saved was gradually abandoned. When they had gone a long time without food, then Paul stood up in their midst and said, "Men, you ought to have followed my advice and not to have set sail from Crete and incurred this damage and loss. Yet now I urge you to keep up your courage, for there will be no loss of life among you, but only of the ship. For this very night an angel of the God to whom I belong and whom I serve stood before me, saying, 'Do not be afraid, Paul; you must stand before Caesar; and behold, God has granted you all those who are sailing with you.' Therefore, keep up your courage, men, for I believe God that it will turn out exactly as I have been told."
Acts 27:20-25 (NASB1995)

Paul continually inspires me during this story. He is on the way to Rome, and his ship has been battling a storm. The pagan crew has prayed to their false gods, and they have not been saved. The boat is going to sink; the despair is palpable. Paul is a mere prisoner and has no earthly authority over these men but still speaks with boldness. He is not afraid to tell them they were wrong not to listen to his advice to delay departure. He also does not keep the good news that they will all be saved to himself. Instead, Paul takes advantage of the opportunity to share his faith and the power of God with others. He does not cower or retreat but leads in the storm.

I wish I were more like Paul, but sadly, especially in the storms of school life, I retreat and let the wind toss the ship. After a meeting about staff layoffs or new testing standards, I don't share the hope I have in Christ with my coworkers. I don't share the indescribable peace that whatever happens in this world He will always be with me and care for me. I don't take the time to encourage others by stories of God's endless faithfulness to me. I neglect to mention that their false securities and false gods can't save them but that the one true God is never far. I don't implore them to find the soul-anchoring reality of Jesus' love. Instead, while my coworkers are stressed and tossed about, I let them weather the storm alone. I'm at peace as they sink into despair.

God has given us His Spirit, and with His strength, we all can be examples of how to handle adversity. Please pray with me for opportunities and the courage to consistently lead in the storm. May God use your example and courage to draw your coworkers to Himself.

Week 17 Day 1
Simplicity of the Gospel Part 1

For Christ did not send me to baptize but to preach the gospel, and not with words of eloquent wisdom, lest the cross of Christ be emptied of its power.
1 Corinthians 1:17 (ESV)

When I was just starting teaching, I was very aware of the common objections to Christianity. Part of my faith journey involved a heavy reading into apologetics to help me understand the reasons for faith. I was hooked. I watched debates between famous Christian apologists and atheists, taking notes on how to respond to doubters of the Gospel. I felt prepared to refute any questions from my students. In fact, I secretly wanted a student to ask a question so that I could go off on a fifteen-minute rebuttal that would leave them convinced and speechless. I saw myself on the intellectual frontlines of battle and felt confident that all my years of preparation and studying had led me to this moment. Bring it on, atheist students, prepare to be debated into the kingdom!

However, when I came across this Scripture, I realized my view of the power of apologetics was unbiblical. Although apologetics is important, Paul mentions here that the cross's real power is not in compelling and convincing arguments but in the cross itself. Paul emphasizes that he purposely preached without words of eloquent wisdom. Rather than enhancing the cross, persuasive words actually detract from the authority of Christ. Paul even says that the cross is emptied of its power if we surround it with too much eloquence. It is not in our ability to communicate by our own wisdom but through the simplicity of the Gospel message that hearts are changed. I needed (and continue to need) to step back and preach the Gospel and rely on the power of the cross to transform my students.

The Gospel does not need to be surrounded by complicated and sophisticated arguments; its effectiveness is in its simplicity. first time I did this, I was amazed at the selfishness of

Week 17 Day 2
Simplicity of the Gospel Part 2
For the message of the cross is foolishness to those who are perishing, but to us who are being saved it is the power of God.
1 Corinthians 1:18 (NIV)

Picking up from yesterday, this idea of focusing on the simplicity of the Gospel was challenging in my Honors Philosophy class. One of the skills students were required to demonstrate was comparing complex arguments from many philosophical thinkers. Additionally, I was teaching incredibly bright students who were all very evidence-based in their thinking. As good thinkers, they wanted evidence for every idea. Here I was confronted with yesterday's devotion. I needed to trust in the simplicity of the Gospel, but it didn't seem to work. I would repeatedly explain the reality of our sin condition and the remedy of the cross, but students were not being converted. I was confused. Maybe I was making things too eloquent?

So, I explained the Gospel in the simplest way possible. Still, no one was convinced. I was frustrated. I was trusting in the power of the cross but was not seeing any fruit. Why were these students so hostile? Why were they making incredible demands for proof of God that no man could answer? I wanted them to critique arguments, but why wasn't God's grace melting hearts? Why were these students rejecting the good news that I have found and experienced?

This verse answers these questions. This Scripture's word choice is compelling, especially when teaching a class full of smart students. In their sin and pride, my students rejected the cross as being silly and stupid. The cross became the antithesis of everything they valued. They were smart and logical. Why would they be attracted to the simple and ridiculous? This was a reality that I could not change. Despite their need for Christ, they would view the cross as foolish until God changed their hearts.

We also see that the cross has absolute power, but its power is not seen by those who are perishing. It's not that the Gospel was impotent in my classroom but that my students were blind to it. Sadly, some of our students are so dead in their sin that the lens through which they see the cross hides its power and beauty. This perspective caused me not to be frustrated at my students but to pray specifically for them. God must move mightily and make dry bones come alive. He is the only remedy for their condition. He must give them new eyes to see. Put simply, I must again rely on the cross and the power of Christ to change hearts.

Oh, teachers, I pray that our students' souls would drive us to our knees every night. Our primary weapon is prayer. God alone can remove the barriers to the Gospel. I pray that my students will not regard the cross as foolish but as beautiful. I pray they find the One they mock as their Savior.

Week 17 Day 3
Simplicity of the Gospel Part 3

For it is written: "I will destroy the wisdom of the wise; the intelligence of the intelligent I will frustrate." Where is the wise person? Where is the teacher of the law? Where is the philosopher of this age? Has not God made foolish the wisdom of the world?
1 Corinthians 1:19-20 (NIV)

God is mighty to save, and I pray He awakens every one of my students. In this age of "New Atheism," you can't turn on the TV without hearing someone blaspheming God and disparaging Christians. These anti-god icons worship their intellect. They believe that they have it all figured out—that they are smarter than their Creator. They weave together complicated arguments in hopes that their verbose vocabulary will win them the debate. They belittle Christians as stupid and inferior. Faith is described as something for the weak and unintelligent. It can be tempting to wonder if they are right. Do they have it all figured out? Can God be disproved with complex arguments? Am I dumb to believe in Him?

I sometimes see my students touting arguments against Christ that seem sophisticated. Their skepticism allows them to skirt arguments and realities while giving them a false sense of intellectual superiority. However, God is not confined by rational arguments. His will and existence are not frustrated by the philosophies of man. The real Author of wisdom is and will be victorious.

These final verses, however, compare the strength of human wisdom against the cross. We see that the cross alone is powerful and that the perishing regard the cross as foolish. Here we see that that is precisely how God has planned salvation; this is precisely His goal. God wants to shame the wise. The Gospel is not an intellectual prize to earn, something only available to those who solve the puzzle. Instead, the Gospel is simple: a free gift of grace, unearned and unmerited. He destroys the wisdom of the wise. There is no one wise compared to the Lord. They have no ground to stand on compared to Him. His plans are better and higher than any human can even fathom. God will frustrate the pretend wisdom of the wise. God gets the final say.

I am in awe of His power and claim to ultimate authority. I am also comforted that He is victorious, and we are as well. In the end, the "wise" opinions about God and about Christians do not matter and will fail. We can rejoice that God reigns and will destroy all claims against Him. We don't have to win every debate; God will defend Himself. He fights every battle. We can boldly speak the simplicity of the cross, knowing that we preach the truth. God will vindicate Himself and us. Before the judgment throne, as we all behold His glory, all of the mocking and ridicule will turn to praise as every knee will bow to Christ and admit that He is Lord. The victory has and will always belong to Him.

There is hope! Our God wins.

Week 18 Day 1
Work Out

For physical training is of some value, but godliness has value for all things, holding promise for both the present life and the life to come.
1 Timothy 4:8 (NIV)

Our world is flooded with get-fit-quick schemes. Shortcuts are advertised everywhere to get into shape and stay thin. We often know what dietary and lifestyle choices to make to improve our health. And although we are bombarded with maintaining our physical fitness, we often don't value our spiritual health on the same level. However, Scripture corrects this error. We can see from this verse that the two aren't even comparable. Physical fitness will give us more energy and a healthier life, but that is all it can bring. Once we reach a certain age, and especially once we die, all of those days at the gym will not benefit us anymore.

However, our spiritual well-being gives us incalculable blessings. During our time on earth, we are nearer to the Lord day by day. We grow in Him and get to enjoy Him more and more. As our intimacy with Him strengthens, we see more and more of His kingdom coming into our lives. Our families, colleagues, students, and loved ones also benefit as the glory of the Lord reflects off of us. And then, when we go home, we can be encouraged that training up in godliness yields results in eternity. Why would we not invest our time and energy into our spiritual health, which will benefit us now and forever?

Physical training is essential to steward our bodies and our health well. God has given you your health, and we must regularly exercise and eat well. To disregard our physical health is to dishonor God. But the 5k that you ran will not profit you as much as consistent prayer and fasting. Righteousness has value for all things. Focus more on eternal training and not only on the temporary and fleeting results of physical fitness.

Week 18 Day 2

Equality

Rich and poor have this in common: The LORD is the Maker of them all.
Proverbs 22:2 (NIV)

About this time of the year, we begin to understand our students pretty well. We know their academic and behavioral habits, as well as their many vices and virtues. If we aren't careful, we can start treating our students differently. I have to stop myself from treating students based on how they act. I might show favoritism to a student who always does well on tests and sometimes ignore the student who tries to sleep in class or is always late.

Favoritism got many families in trouble in the Bible and goes against our role as a shepherd of our students. Every student in your classroom is made in the image of God. All students have intrinsic value since they are all created by God. Even the challenging students were consciously, creatively, and uniquely made by Him. In times of struggling with favoritism, I have to remember that all my students were thoughtfully created.

Love all your students because their worth is not based on how they act but Who their Maker is.

Week 18 Day 3
Raised to Life

And you, who were dead in your trespasses and the uncircumcision of your flesh, God made alive together with him, having forgiven us all our trespasses, by canceling the record of debt that stood against us with its legal demands. This he set aside, nailing it to the cross.
Colossians 2:13-14 (ESV)

The more I mature, by God's grace, the more I find that the Gospel has a rejuvenating power in my life. God's transformation in making me born again was even more miraculous than I initially realized. I'm comforted when I see so many students rejecting God because I am reminded that I was just like them. The good news gives me hope for myself and the success of God's kingdom.

Here in Colossians, we are told that before Christ, we were dead in our transgressions. Our sin did not just make us sick or mortally wounded but completely dead. We were hopeless, incapable of life or loving God. Our sins were so great that we could never get rid of them. We could never have fellowship with God.

We were all Lazarus, dead in the tomb until Jesus intervened. When Jesus shows up and does the impossible, He raises the dead. He creates life where there was no life. When Jesus defeated death, it was a great shout that called us from the grave and made us alive. In raising us from death, He took the entire record of our debt and fulfilled the payment on the cross. He nailed our hell-bound future to the cross and nullified our guilty sentence. There is now no sin that can be held against us. There is no wrong that Jesus did not make right.

Fresh reminders of His unearned love motivate me to better live out my faith before my students and my family at home.

Don't let the enemy lie to you and tell you that Christ died for most of your sins. No, He died for every single sin—past, present, and future. Jesus said so as He died—"It is finished"—and He meant it. He has forgiven us of all our trespasses and raised us from the dead. You were not beyond His grace; your deadness in sin was not too much an obstacle for Him. He loved you, so He saved you.

This same resurrecting power can still happen to your students. Their deadness is not an obstacle for Christ. Jesus just has to speak one word, and your students will be raised up. Pray for them!

Be encouraged by the Gospel in your own life and let it motivate you all the more in your classroom and beyond.

Last Day of the Semester: Meditate on the Lord

But since you refuse to listen when I call and no one pays attention when I stretch out my hand, since you disregard all my advice and do not accept my rebuke, I in turn will laugh when disaster strikes you; I will mock when calamity overtakes you—when calamity overtakes you like a storm, when disaster sweeps over you like a whirlwind, when distress and trouble overwhelm you.
Proverbs 1:24-27 (NIV)

This warning paints a bleak picture of what will happen if we don't listen to the Lord. It is, therefore, crucial to spend specific time seeking the Lord's counsel. Proverbs remind us here of the importance of listening to God throughout our journey. When we turn a deaf ear to His instruction, any storm we go through will be exponentially worse without Him. This isn't about do's and don'ts but about loving the Lord enough to seek and obey His counsel. It only takes a few moments of thinking about how much more wise He is than us for us to run to His wisdom.

Going into Christmas break, take the time to spend concentrated and focused time with the Lord in prayer. Prayerfully reflect on the semester. Celebrate the victories and bring to the Lord the things that grieved you. Thank Him for His providence and ask for His favor and guidance during the second semester. Ask for His help to obey His advice and not to despise His rebuke.
Enjoy His presence and be rejuvenated when you return to school.

SEMESTER 2

Week 19 Day 1
Not Innocent but Ignorant
I thought, "These are only the poor; they are foolish, for they do not know the way of the LORD, *the requirements of their God."*
Jeremiah 5:4 (NIV)

One day in my classroom, I was walking around monitoring as students worked on group projects. As they worked, they talked to each other. They thought they were whispering, but I heard everything loud and clear, and I couldn't believe my ears. The things that they had recently seen, done, heard about, and wanted to do the next weekend genuinely shocked me.

They were all way too young and, I thought, too innocent to say the things I heard come from their mouths. I was disheartened to listen to the glorified, unashamed sin that was bragged about. The first reaction of my heart was to get angry at them. How could you so flagrantly dishonor God? How could you revel in sin? I wanted to flip tables like Jesus did in the Temple.

My next thought was to sink into hopelessness and despair. These sixteen-year-olds were so steeped in debauchery, how could they ever be set free? How could they ever come to Christ?

Later, the Lord brought me to this verse, and I realized my heart was wrong. Although all people have a general revelation of God and understand basic morality, these students were ignorant of God's law. It was clear that they had never been to church.

They didn't have a loving, godly adult shape them by God's Word. Again, they were not innocent. Scripture is clear that we are all sinful and have enough knowledge to be held accountable, but these students were ignorant of God's law. They were not aware that the major benefit of God's law is to reveal our need for a Savior. We must see the true depths of our depravity before we can turn to Christ. Then, when we are confronted with all it takes to be righteous before God, we know that we are hopeless unless Jesus intervenes. Therefore, the hour of our greatest shame becomes the hour of our greatest joy.

Consequently, one of the greatest prayers we can pray over our students is that their knowledge of God will increase, and His undeniable grace will compel them to righteousness. Instead of shaking my head in disbelief, I needed to bow my head and pray that they would come to know the Lord and His commandments so that they could find Jesus.

Lord, may You bring the knowledge of Your law into their lives to help get them off this road to destruction. Intervene, O God.

Week 19 Day 2
Jesus: The Greater Passion

And those who belong to Christ Jesus have crucified the flesh with its passions and desires.
Galatians 5:24 (ESV)

This is a simple statement, but it speaks to a grand reality. Paul reminds us that all those belonging to Christ share in this glorious reality. The reality that Christ's death gives us power and freedom to crucify our flesh with all of its passions and desires.

But what does it mean to crucify the flesh with its passions and desires? We first have to remember that we are all born sinners, in the flesh. Our sinful nature is to do what we love, which is to sin. We follow the desires and the passions of our flesh uninhibited. Jesus said that all who sin are slaves to sin. Since we all have sinned, that means we are all slaves to sin. Therefore, we are all in need of a Savior to break the chains that bind us. Sin separates us from God, who is the source and definition of goodness in the universe. Our sinful flesh always overpromises and under-delivers. Sin is a cruel master that promises pleasure but provides destruction.

Secondly, notice what Paul says here in this verse. Crucifying the flesh and sin-killing is not optional for the Christian. Paul doesn't say that some Christians have crucified the flesh and some others live consumed in the flesh. No, all Christians have and must continue to kill sin and its evil desires.

But here's the reality of our natural state: we don't have the strength or ability to kill this sin master on our own. But the unbelievably good news is that we don't crucify our flesh in our own power. Jesus has given all Christians His Spirit. The Holy Spirit provides us with the desire and ability to kill the sin in our lives and to grow in holiness. One of His many roles in our lives is to make us more like Christ, so He is on our side. He will help you kill sin.

To fight this continual war, you must choose the greater desire of holiness compared to the shallow desires of sin. Our love for Jesus must be stronger than our love for our flesh. And as we grow in holiness, we can more brightly reflect God's glory to our students and those around us.

So be encouraged and fight the war with our King on our side.

Week 19 Day 3
God's Timing, God's Strength

Humble yourselves, therefore, under the mighty hand of God so that at the proper time he may exalt you.
1 Peter 5:6 (ESV)

We all know that teaching has a political side. We have genuine relationships with those in authority and power over us. However, I always wanted a little more. If I wasn't in the inner circle of decision making, I wanted to get there as soon as possible.

To do this, I routinely "played the game" and didn't think anything of it. I would try extra hard to find something to talk about or find things I had in common with those in authority. I always wanted to be seen doing my job well and being a good teacher. This would hopefully earn respect, which would lead to further conversations. During those conversations, I would try to bring up classes I wanted to teach or extracurricular duties I wanted to change for the next year. I would play this off as just chatting, but in my heart, I was planting seeds I wanted to see come to fruition.

As Christians, we are not to be caught up in trying to orchestrate situations or influence people for our gain. In doing so, we try to secure our own future in our own timing. This narrow-minded, prideful manipulation boils down to a lack of faith on our part.

Do we trust our future to God? If we do, why go around planting seeds? Why do our actions resemble a master planner instead of an obedient servant? Do we really know what's best for ourselves? If we want His will for our lives, then why do we go about putting our own plan into action?

Scripture here tells us to put our pride to death and submit our plans and future to God. When we humble ourselves under His mighty hand, two things happen. One, we remain under His protection, which is the best place to be. Two, He promises to raise us up at the proper time. Don't skip over that. At the literal perfect time, the God who created the heavens and earth will lift you up. With God for you, who can be against you? You will succeed in His strength and with His help. Isn't that what we want? Don't we want to be successful and bear much fruit? If so, we can't create our own fruit in our own timing. There is no better time and no better support to have than the Lord. If we don't submit and instead try to stand on our own, we will not thrive but fall.

So have genuine friendships and relationships with those in authority. Have conversations relating to your job, but never try to take things into your own hands. Humble yourself. Trust God. He knows what He is doing.

Week 20 Day 1
Paradigm Shift
If we endure, we will also reign with him; if we deny him, he also will deny us.
2 Timothy 2:12 (ESV)

Often, I get so focused on the day-to-day and demanding deadlines of our profession that I lose sight of what matters; I lose sight of eternity. One event opened my eyes to this and fundamentally shook me to my core.

In our school, we required all graduating seniors to make a presentation on their high school career in front of their friends, teachers, parents, and faculty. Included in this presentation was a ten-minute explanation of the student's worldview. One year we had a student raised in a Christian home spend ten minutes forcefully renouncing her faith. We had heard rumors of her journey through seas of doubt, and I had heard her increasingly hostile rhetoric toward Christ in my philosophy class, but nothing could have prepared us for the extent of her abandonment of the faith. Heartbreaking doesn't even begin to describe it.

She talked about how her faith was shattered after reading Darwin and Dawkins. She couldn't believe a God existed since the Big Bang proved the universe's creation without God. She also thought prayer had been debunked by science and claimed that the Holy Spirit was just a psychological construct made by those too weak to deal with life on their own. It was so difficult to hear. I could feel the Holy Spirit grieving as she lectured us on the stupidity of our belief. As she continued, I pitied her. Here she was, confidently, proudly, and publicly denying her Creator. She mocked Christ, her only hope for salvation. At the end of the presentation, it was so quiet that you could hear a pin drop. She smiled, beaming with blaspheme.

After her presentation, my spirit was so heavy that a weight remained on my heart for several weeks after. Everything I was so concerned with a day ago—getting my grades caught up, answering emails, lesson planning—seemed so useless, so temporal. My grade book would pass away, as will everything I have ever said, but the Word of the Lord will remain. His Word and the eternal destination of all of my students is what will last forever. Had I done all I could for that student? Did I accurately model and preach Christ? How much more must I pray for my students' conversions? How much more do I tremble when I consider the responsibility of witnessing to them? How much more should I be concerned with their souls and not just their behavior and academic performances?

I don't know what has happened to this former student. Truly no one is beyond God's grace, and no heart of stone is impossible for God to soften. I pray the Lord calls her and draws her to Himself. I pray she repents and finds in Him more than she ever could have imagined. I also pray that I never lose sight of eternity, for nothing in this career, or our life, will last.

Week 20 Day 2
The Lord Determines Our Steps
The heart of man plans his way, but the LORD *establishes his steps.*
Proverbs 16:9 (ESV)

This verse is similar to a previous entry with a more specific application. I have been slow to learn this lesson of trusting the Lord and not my own plans. I am convinced more than ever that we must listen closely to the Lord's will every day and remain humble during every bump and turn of our careers. Don't fall into the temptation of planning a career move or significant change without first being sure you are acting in obedience.

I made this mistake once. It was November, and I was confident that I would be going to a different school the next year. I spent Christmas break planning new classes to teach and even thought about how to tell my students and principal. After the break, I spent my time imagining what a transition would look like, and I became disengaged from my current students. I could not focus and couldn't commit 100% to my classroom for the better part of four months; it was awful.

Well, May came, and the position I thought would open up never did. In fact, no other local schools were hiring. This meant that come August, I would still be at my current job.

All my planning was for nothing. God shut that door, and He reminded me that He has the final say. My students deserved an attentive teacher, and I missed the mark. I think back on all the opportunities I may have missed, how many divine appointments I squandered. I didn't honor the Lord by working as diligently as I should have.

I thought of a plan involving a new school, but the Lord directed my steps to stay. This was a painful lesson to learn. I wanted my plans to succeed, but my intentions were not His. However, His plans will always be better than ours. I needed to trust in Who He is and that He will always do things for my good and His glory. Sometimes I just don't see how His decisions will be good for me until later.

Additionally, His control brings such peace from knowing that we don't have to make our own path. We don't need to spend countless hours trying to plan every career move. He loves us and has already planned out every detail. All we need to do is to trust Him in every season and follow the path He has ordained.

Week 20 Day 3
Never Give Up

Let love and faithfulness never leave you; bind them around your neck, write them on the tablet of your heart. Then you will win favor and a good name / in the sight of God and man.
Proverbs 3:3-4 (NIV)

This time of the year is always challenging. Students stop doing homework about this time, grades start slipping, and all the steam you started the year with has evaporated. It can be so easy to fall into the apathy trap that your students have already succumbed to.

Do not lower your standards.

Do not give up on your students.

Do not stop loving them.

You are their teacher and guide. You have more school days to go. That is more days of divine appointments where academic and life lessons await your instruction. If you give up on them now, who will carry the torch?

Be faithful to them as God has been faithful to you.

Week 21 Day 1
Talking

Let your conversation be gracious and attractive so that you will have the right response for everyone.
Colossians 4:6 (NLT)

It was the last day of school full of bittersweet goodbyes with students. A great student who was a joy to teach approached me at the end of class.

As she told me goodbye, she broke down crying and said six words I will never forget:

"I appreciated our conversations so much."

I didn't know what to say. She had just shattered everything I thought I knew about the influence of educators. The last thing she told me was not, "Mr. Way, I'm grateful for your meaningful feedback on my essays," or, "I will never forget your enlightening lecture over the Civil War," but, "Our conversations meant something to me." She elaborated that she had some rough days during the year but that our conversations had brought her hope on those gloomy days.

Was there a deep conversation that I had with her? I racked my brain. Was there a movie moment where the words I spoke changed her life? Nope. I wish I could say I remember what we talked about, but I don't. I mostly engaged in small talk with her before or after class. I could only remember asking how her day was going and what new marches they were learning in band. These conversations seemed trivial to me, but they weren't for her. These conversations were the medium through which God used me. God took my ordinary chats and used them to make an extraordinary impact on her.

You never know how God will use your small acts of love to impact your students. God may give you the exact words a student desperately needs to persevere. Your conversations might be the only thing they look forward to at school. So be sure to listen to and follow the guiding of the Holy Spirit. Some days He may call you to just listen and some days He will give you the words needed. Keep your words seasoned with the Gospel that you may know how to engage every student. Don't be afraid of the ordinary; even the ordinary is ordained.

What a great reminder—God likes to use the unexpected to change the world.

Our subjects, or lesson plans, do not convey the Gospel; our relationships with our students do. Teaching is not the end-all; it is how we show Christ's love. Consequently, students will forget what you taught them quickly, but they will never forget their relationship with you.

Week 21 Day 2
Clothed in Humility
Clothe yourselves, all of you, with humility toward one another, for "God opposes the proud but gives grace to the humble."
1 Peter 5:5 (ESV)

Almost every year, I come back to this verse with a fresh perspective and a constant need to repent and seek humility. When I first started teaching, I had a major reality check. Everything that I learned from textbooks and student teaching was so different from my classroom; I felt isolated and helpless. Thankfully, the Lord used this time to draw me closer to Him. It seemed like every day, I had to genuinely ask for His help to get through the day because I was so incapable. Then, as I grew in confidence, I started to grow in independence. Consequently, I was much less reliant on the Lord.

Before too long, we as teachers can look up at our classrooms and feel immense pride and begin to believe that we have caused the success we enjoy. The beginning of the second semester naturally brings a level of confidence that exceeds the first semester. Therefore, regardless of how many years you have been teaching, the second semester is always easier. I know for me, I invariably develop "second-semester arrogance."

Not long ago you had a great Christmas break; you know all of your students' names, personalities, and learning styles. You are rocking and rolling, ready to generate momentum to carry through until the end of the year. Be careful. Your confidence could be at a dangerous level.

Pride is the root of all sin. It is a declaration that we don't need God. It is no surprise, then, that one thing God requires of us is to walk humbly with Him.

We are called to be humble in all we do and with all we interact with. We put on this humility and wear it around us. Our humility covers us everywhere we go and is a witness to the proud world.

We can't forget where we get our strength and ability. We also must heed the warning that if we remain in our pride, God opposes us. If you are too prideful, God will work against you, and you will lose.

Conversely, if you are humble, you will receive His grace. Ask for His help today. Perhaps you pray less than you did four months ago. Start fixing that. Remind yourself that you are powerless without Him. Affirm to God that you need Him today just as much as that first day of school.

Do all that you can to clothe yourself in humility. Turn second-semester arrogance into second-semester humility.

Week 21 Day 3
Play Your Part
I planted the seed, Apollos watered it, but God has been making it grow. So neither the one who plants nor the one who waters is anything, but only God, who makes things grow. The one who plants and the one who waters have one purpose, and they will each be rewarded according to their own labor. For we are co-workers in God's service; you are God's field, God's building.
1 Corinthians 3:6-9 (NIV)

Being a teacher means wearing several hats and keeping lots of plates spinning at once. In addition to our professional and personal lives, we are also called to lead our students spiritually. The weight of carrying all of these roles can easily weigh us down.

I remember one week being so overwhelmed by this myriad of responsibilities that I broke down in a panic attack at home. How can I teach my kids to increase their reading level by three years, help them pass their state tests, inspire them to overcome their home lives, and demonstrate the love of the Father, all the while doing my best to model Christ to every student every day? There's no way I can do it all. How could I even do two of these things well? Even one? I felt destined for failure.

The Holy Spirit then brought these verses to me and immediately His peace washed over me. God has not called us to do everything and be everything for our students. God has called us only to accomplish the task He assigns. We don't have to plant, water, prune, grow, and harvest. We don't have to do it all; we just have to play our part. All we have to do is our task; this was a liberating reality.

God will give you wisdom and opportunities. We may scatter seeds for one student, water a little for another, and prune fruit from another. We won't see the final product, but ultimately the outcome is being orchestrated and sustained by God. Trust that God will use your contribution as a piece of the overall story of each student you have. Don't worry; you don't have to accomplish everything for everyone. Just fulfill your role. God will complete His purposes, and His success is not dependent on anyone.

Instead of being stressed, enjoy being used by Him. All you need to do is faithfully and prayerfully serve and trust Him for the rest.

Week 22 Day 1
Messianic Obedience

For I have come down from heaven not to do my will but to do the will of him who sent me.
John 6:38 (NIV)

If anyone in history had the right to live on earth as they saw fit, it was Jesus Christ. Firstly, He created all things. In eternity past, in His infinite wisdom, He chose to make the world and all that inhabits it. Secondly, He experienced perfect communion with the Father in the Holy Spirit and enjoyed the praise and worship owed to Him in heaven. Ever since He created the angels and heavenly hosts, they have been praising Him for who He is. They have adored and loved Him. They reflect His glory, and their praise is tangible proof of His magnificence. Jesus left this elevated status and took on the form of a man and lived among His creation. On earth, He had the power to do all that he wanted and could have been worshiped as He was in heaven. Instead, He was mocked, ridiculed, and blasphemed. He endured the irreverence that resulted in the damnation of Satan and his followers.

However, Christ didn't assert His rightful reign over His creatures. He did not carry out His own will but submitted to the will of the Father.

Wow.

Jesus, a distinct person of the Trinity, forfeits His kingly prerogative to submit to the Father completely. How do we usually respond to God's authority?

To submit, we must die to our own preferences to obey the Father. We must forgo whatever we feel entitled to and serve Him. No matter the cost, we must joyfully submit. If the Son of Man willingly obeyed the Father, how much more should we, His creation, humble ourselves before our Creator? Christ's perfect submission is both an example of the utmost humility and our example to follow.

May we never take the will of God lightly, and may we do our best to mirror Christ's obedience in our professional and personal lives.

Week 22 Day 2
Blessed Forgiveness

Blessed is the one whose transgressions are forgiven, whose sins are covered. . . .Then I acknowledged my sin to you and did not cover up my iniquity. I said, "I will confess my transgressions to the LORD." And you forgave the guilt of my sin.
Psalm 32:1, 5 (NIV)

I often take forgiveness for granted. I need this reminder that forgiveness is always a blessing. We should never become complacent toward Christ's forgiveness of all our sins. God's grace is not cheap. Jesus paid the high price for our forgiveness by being punished for every sin we have committed and will commit. His death and resurrection give us the ability and assurance that He will forgive us our sins every time we confess.

God poured His grace out on us, not because we are good but only because He loved us. We are not entitled to mercy. Mercy is not what we deserve; hell is.

We should not arrogantly go one day without confessing our transgressions against the Lord.

Search your heart today. Ask the Lord to reveal any unconfessed sins and then ask forgiveness.

He will always forgive your sins, and then you can rejoice in the blessing that your sin is covered.

Thank you, Jesus!

Week 22 Day 3
A Sustaining Word
The Sovereign Lord has given me a well-instructed tongue, to know the word that sustains the weary. He wakens me morning by morning, wakens my ear to listen like one being instructed.
Isaiah 50:4 (NIV)

The longer I teach, the more I realize the power our words have with students. This reality used to fill me with confidence, but the more I consider the weight of my words, the heavier I feel my responsibility is.

To give this type of sustaining word, described by Isaiah, we cannot rely on our wisdom and timing. We must be receptive and listening to the Lord. Then, in His sovereignty, He prepares our hearts and gives us the words that our students need to hear. This is a powerful gift God gives to our students. In fact, a God-ordained conversation with students can change eternal trajectories.

I have had the joy of being a part of these moments. There was a unique pattern that emerged. First, the Lord would randomly bring a former student to mind. This was often so out of the blue that I was sure that it was from the Lord. Then, the Holy Spirit burdened me to pray for them. I wouldn't know what to pray, but He would direct my thoughts. I wouldn't always pray immediately, but He was patient with me and helped me to recognize these moments.

Later on, almost without fail, I would get an email or a surprise visit from the student I had prayed for. Each conversation with them always involved them seeking advice, desperately craving direction, or needing encouragement and affirmation.

During and after each conversation, I had such a strong sense of the Lord's guiding hand. He gave me the words to say and how to say them. Afterward, He gave me just a glimpse of His having moved in a powerful way. I had a real sense of awe after those moments. I wish I could tell you the specifics of how all of those conversations went or even what I said, but I don't remember. I do know that after every discussion, I was grateful to the Lord that I had prayed beforehand.

It's funny; when I first became a teacher, I imagined these types of life-changing discussions would happen all the time. Seven years later, I know that they don't. There are countless moments in which the Lord uses us each year, but the ones we see and are aware of are limited. However, we need to be continually praying for them so that when the Lord brings them to us, we are aware of the Holy Spirit and rely on Him for the words to speak to our students. He will help you. He will use you to speak powerfully and influence students for His glory.

Week 23 Day 1
The Stress of My Students' Salvation Part 1
All those the Father gives me will come to me, and whoever comes to me I will never drive away.
John 6:37 (NIV)

This verse came to me amid incredible stress and anguish. I was teaching a philosophy class, and day in and day out, my heart broke to see so many of my students reject Christ. Even arguments for theism were spat upon, and the name of Jesus was said with disrespect and disdain. I was so frustrated that the hearts of my students were so hard and resistant.

Their rejection made me overwhelmed about the task of witnessing to them. I saw such little progress in so many conversations. If my purpose here was to minister, then I was failing. The weight of the severity of my students' rebellion grieved me. In this state, I read these words of Jesus, and He righted my thinking about salvation and brought me assurance and peace.

Jesus states that all that the Father gives Him will come to Him. Even if I preached all day and lectured on apologetics all night, I would not convince someone to believe in Christ in my own power. It is not up to me to bring them to Jesus. I don't have to convince them or drag them kicking and screaming to Jesus. Their saving faith is not a byproduct of my effort. No debate or catchy phrase will turn my students to Jesus; that is only the work of the Lord. If

God desires to save one of your students, He will draw them to Jesus, and that student will come. This means that God's success rate with unbelievers is 100%.

I often, wrongly, link my success as a Christian teacher to how many students I can mentor or what percentage of students I can lead to Christ. This inevitably leads to frustration and a sense of failure. As I have grown, I have seen that holding myself to this unrealistic standard is not supported by Scripture. Your students,' administrators,' colleagues,' and family members' salvation is not dependent on you. Yes, we pray that God may use us to achieve this purpose, but the burden of saving the lost is not yours to bear. Our job is to preach, testify, and be witnesses, but God will call them, and Christ will receive them.

Pray for opportunities to witness and thank God that all He calls will come. Nothing can stop our God!

Week 23 Day 2
The Stress of My Students' Salvation Part 2

All those the Father gives me will come to me, and whoever comes to me I will never drive away.
John 6:37 (NIV)

Picking up from yesterday, another revealing truth about salvation is stated in the second half of this verse. I am comforted that all those who come to Jesus will not be driven away. If a student approaches Christ, He welcomes them with open arms. He will not drive any away. You don't have to convince someone to come to Christ and then pray the Lord accepts them. My role as a teacher is not to draw students to Christ but to point them to Him.

Don't burden yourself with an unbiblical view of your role. Fulfill your purpose, and God will achieve His. Salvation is His business, and He has a perfect record of accomplishing His plans. What great news! If the salvation of our students were up to us, we would fail them completely. That pressure is too much to comprehend. However, He will never fail them. We can witness in confidence and trust God to draw His children to Jesus.

The glorious conclusion to this reality is this: Jesus will not drive away or reject anyone who comes to Him. If the Father calls a student, Jesus will receive him or her. How magnificent, how incredible! Jesus will accept all people who come to Him. All who seek will find. All who thirst for righteousness in Him will be filled.

God is both able and powerful enough to make this true.

This morning, rejoice in God's omniscience, power, and might to save.

Week 23 Day 3

The Stress of My Students' Salvation Part 3

I give them eternal life, and they shall never perish; no one will snatch them out of my hand. My Father, who has given them to me, is greater than all; no one can snatch them out of my Father's hand. I and the Father are one.
John 10:28-30 (NIV)

Another component of the stress of my role in the salvation of my students was, If they did become Christians in a nurturing, Christian environment, how could their faith survive secular college and beyond?

If the miracle of salvation occurred, how could a student grow in faith away from Christian adults and mentors? If a student is born again as a sophomore, there is plenty of time to build them up, but if a second-semester senior becomes a believer, are they destined to have weak faith and no fruit? Would they apostatize later? What must I do as a teacher to ensure my new-believing students become mature in their faith?

Again, the Lord used His word to calm my fears and answer my questions. I was again convicted by the answers to these questions found in John 10. It is Jesus, not Christian mentors, who gives eternal life. Just as salvation was not dependent on me, the perseverance of all Christians is also not up to me. Christ will keep all those called to Him. No amount of effort on our parts will ever achieve what Christ did on the cross.

Likewise, my fear of training them before they entered the secular world was also unbiblical. Every believer, including brand-new Christians, is secure in the Father's hand. They are eternally safe there. No one can snatch them away—no secular college, no hardship, nothing. God is greater than all, and He alone keeps all who belong to Him. What an incredibly humbling and convicting truth. I thought too highly of myself and the influence of Christian mentors to believe that we alone could ensure students remained in the faith. We can mold and shape, but we do not secure their salvation; God does that for all of His children.

Indeed, to better pray and minister to our students, we must have a biblical understanding of God's role in salvation. Our opinions of ourselves must decrease so that we may see the elevated reality of His role in keeping us.

Thank Him today that you are forever safe in His hands.

Week 24 Day 1
Joy from the Lord

You have put more joy in my heart / than they have when their grain and wine abound.
Psalm 4:7 (ESV)

Teaching is the most incredible and rewarding profession on earth. I love preparing a thoughtful lesson and seeing my students connect with and learn material every day. I still get goosebumps when I see a student struggle and then come to an understanding right before my eyes. Those "lightbulb" moments are compelling.

Often one "lightbulb" moment gives you the energy to chase for the next one. No matter how few and far between these moments are, they are rewarding and incredibly addicting. I go to work sometimes only in pursuit of that rush. However, it is always humbling to remember that they are not my source of joy, no matter how incredible those moments are. I have to stop myself from chasing the false god of "learning moments." Those moments cannot sustain my soul; they do not speak to my innermost being as my Creator does. My joy comes from the Lord. He fills my heart directly with joy and gladness. And satisfaction in Him is always better than any other temporary pleasure in this world.

He and He alone truly satisfies me. Remember today to find joy in the classroom, but remember the real source of everlasting joy comes from the Lord.

Week 24 Day 2
Truth About Complaining

Do everything without grumbling or arguing, so that you may become blameless and pure, "children of God without fault in a warped and crooked generation." Then you will shine among them like stars in the sky.
Philippians 2:14-15 (NIV)

This verse always convicts me. No matter what time of day or year, I often find myself complaining. For me, this is easiest to do at school with other teachers, even in passing in the hallways. Lesson plans, students, an impromptu assembly—the list is endless. Because we have so many unexpected things that bombard us throughout the day, it is easy to take these new responsibilities and tell everyone who will listen how burdensome they are.

However tempting, we as believers cannot complain. Complaining erodes our purity and damages our witness. Ultimately, complaining demonstrates a lack of trust in God's character and His sovereignty.

Nothing happens to us in this life that has not first passed through the hands of the Father. He allows us to only go through challenges that He will use for His glory and our good. Complaining really means complaining about the situation God has orchestrated, about His design and His will. Therefore, when we complain about our circumstances, we are really complaining about God.

Trust God's goodness. We must endure our trials without grumbling so that we come out the other side a brighter and better reflection of Christ, shining like stars.

Week 24 Day 3
Be Grateful

But I trust in your unfailing love; my heart rejoices in your salvation. I will sing the LORD's praise, for he has been good to me.
Psalm 13:5-6 (NIV)

It seems that this time of year there is always something. Testing, lesson plans, students who are still not adhering to classroom expectations, and even the breaking copier all drain your resolve. I also start thinking about how my students will perform on state assessments and how, concurrently, my performance will be judged. If we aren't careful, frustration and exhaustion can plant seeds of bitterness. These seeds can grow and cause you to sin and rob your joy. No matter the stresses of work, we should always rejoice in our countless blessings.

Take the time today to reflect on all that God has done for you. Consider Him providing this job, relationships with administrators and colleagues, your students, and your family. Thank Him for the patience and faithfulness He has shown you all your life. Most importantly, thank Him for the gift of His Son, by and through whom we have salvation. Without Christ, we would be without hope. But God, in His mercy, became a man and died for us. He then rose on the third day giving His people eternal life with Him. Thank you, Lord! His love is limitless—what a wonderful God we serve. Thank Him for who He is and spend the day recognizing all of His blessings.

Week 25 Day 1

Impactful Advice I Don't Remember

In his defense Jesus said to them, "My Father is always at his work to this very day, and I too am working."
John 5:17 (NIV)

One day after class, I was talking with a senior about her future. She was discussing the daunting reality of graduation. She explained the stress of taking a leap into the unknown and choosing a college and future career.

Then she suddenly broke down. She told me I had given her advice in class last year that confirmed her life and career. As tears streamed down her face, she told me how impactful I had been in establishing her desire to become a teacher. She had been doubting her calling but was now committed to pursuing her dream. As she told me this, I racked my brain, trying to remember what I told her. I couldn't remember any specific conversation, even though it was only eight months ago.

When she left, I was beaming. I had changed her life. My brilliant advice helped her become a teacher. I had changed the trajectory of her life. Wow, I must be the teacher of the century! I asked the Lord what conversation she was referring to. I thought I should write down that advice and be prepared for the next student who needs me. But God didn't bring any advice to mind. He only answered me in the conviction of my inflated ego. It's a wonder I could

walk through my door with how big my head was.
How quick I was to praise myself and disregard God.
My pride needed to be checked.

After I asked forgiveness, God still didn't bring to
mind the piece of advice. However, despite my feeling
frustrated, the Lord began teaching me that my
forgetting this advice was really an answered prayer. I
pray for those powerful words to speak to students
because I can't cause them. If I had a set of eloquent
lines prepared to tell students, then I wouldn't be
relying on God at all.

Most of the time, I go through each day anticipating
these divine conversations as if they will be very
formal and overt. While a few of these have
happened, that is not the norm. In fact, what is more
common is for the Spirit to speak through me in such
a way that I do not know that what I said was
meaningful. Only after the fact do students come to
me and mention something.

The more this happens, the more I am convinced this
is best because God gets all the glory. I don't
remember what I said, so I can remain humble and
not reliant on worldly wisdom. I can never remember
the advice, so I don't dole it out to students with
expectations of its impact. Nor could I say anything
of value in my own strength. I have to rely on the
Lord. I am utterly dependent on Him. For my good, I
shouldn't remember my advice so that I won't swell
with pride. I remain reliant on the Spirit for wisdom
and not myself. It is for God's glory also that I don't
remember so that I rely on Him, and He gets all the

credit.

I'm also grateful that God shows me these instances to remind me that He answers my prayers. He is using me. These are brief glimpses but mean so much to me. My faith is strengthened, and I am encouraged to pray more boldly. My soul is lifted to know that He is always moving, even when I don't see any fruit.

So be hopeful. Pray for times for the Lord to speak to your students and trust that He is, even if you don't remember it.

Week 25 Day 2
God's Kingdom will Succeed
And the Lord said to Paul one night in a vision, "Do not be afraid, but go on speaking and do not be silent, for I am with you, and no one will attack you to harm you, for I have many in this city who are my people." And he stayed a year and six months, teaching the word of God among them.
Acts 18:9-11 (ESV)

I remember looking out from my desk at all my students. From a recent discussion, I knew that I had only one professing Christian sitting in a desk before me. How many Christians would be in my class next year? And what about the year after that? Would there be any Christians in my class in the future? What if I never taught another Christian student again? Would the Holy Spirit move again? Would I see evidence of Him in our student body?

Not long after this, the Lord brought me to this story in Acts. Paul has just been beaten for sharing the Gospel and wasn't seeing much fruit either. Then the Lord tells Paul not to be afraid because He had "many in this city who are my people." Wow! What an incredible revelation of hope and encouragement from the Lord. The Lord knows who His people are, and there are many in the city! Some of them have not yet been revealed, but they are there. God has planned for the success of His kingdom. His people are everywhere. In every country and classroom around the world, God knows who His people are. After hearing this, Paul changes his plans and stays for a year teaching and growing these believers.

I began to see my students and my future through a different lens. I looked over my students believing that the Lord had His people in my class and our school. We don't know them yet, and maybe some of them will have to be a little older, but they belong to Him nevertheless. Don't give up and become hopeless. We persevere and trust that the Lord has planned for His success. And we believe that His people are among us, whether we recognize them or not.

Week 25 Day 3
Our Perseverance is a Witness
Let your forbearance be known unto all men. The Lord is at hand.
Philippians 4:5 (ASV)

I had a challenging semester. Attending grad school, trying to tame rowdy freshmen, and more school responsibilities with less time to accomplish them. I felt like I was always swimming upstream. It was easy under these circumstances to complain to other teachers and lament about everything that was happening. It was even easier to lie to myself and justify my behavior. I told myself, "I know I'm complaining all the time, but I'm building rapport with my peers. This will help me witness better in the future!" We can justify sin so quickly, can't we?

Wallowing in misery and strife is not strengthening your witness. Sin is never a good example. Instead, God tells us that our patience and forbearance through trial and persecution is what acts as our witness. It is because we have the Spirit that we can withstand the challenges we face. This is a testimony to the world because they can't understand our joy in trial and the strength to thrive in challenges. Our perseverance then acts as a way to demonstrate how a Christian responds and lives in adversity. Our reliance on Him helps others see the reality that God is at hand.

He is here, and He is with us. Live this truth, and let the whole world see Him.

Week 26 Day 1

Modeling Christian Confrontation

If your brother sins against you, go and tell him his fault, between you and him alone. If he listens to you, you have gained your brother.
Matthew 18:15 (ESV)

I once had a significant disagreement with a student. Some miscommunication led to a public conflict in the middle of an all-school meeting. Basically, I had to correct a student about some information that they were announcing to the student body. This student was in front with a microphone, and I was standing in the audience. Both of us were openly disagreeing with each other in front of everyone. It was awkward, to say the least.

I knew that I needed to reconcile with this student; what happened was not the best way to handle the situation. I had embarrassed her, and there was palpable tension between us. But since I was the adult, and I was also correct in the argument, I became further entrenched in my stubbornness. I'm sad to admit it, but I let my pride get the best of me. I refused to apologize for most of the day. The Lord convicted me two times to speak with the student, and I was disobedient both times. Thankfully, He gave one last opportunity before the end of the day, and I obeyed.

The Lord was gracious and really worked in the conversation, and He brought us both to a place of understanding. I was grateful to have obeyed the Lord and saw the benefit of initiating that hard conversation with that student. Sometime later, I heard from that student's parents that they appreciated my effort since they were believers. They were encouraged to see Christians resolving conflict biblically. They said it was a teachable moment for their child to see an adult obeying biblical principles in the real world. I was too embarrassed to tell them that I disobeyed twice before I did, but I was grateful for the encouragement.

I was then struck with the reality of what had happened. Not only should we handle conflict biblically and obey Christ out of our love for Him, but God also uses these opportunities to strengthen His Church. When the Church treats each other as God has called us to, our faith grows.

With this situation, a student, her parents, and I were all encouraged in our faith. The Lord used this one event to teach several people a valuable lesson. We all got to experience the joy of obedience to Christ together. These are the benefits we miss out on when we don't act with courage toward our students. Had I remained afraid and not obeyed, then the Lord couldn't have blessed so many people in this way.

We follow Christ out of devotion to Him and also because we are examples to our students. This is even truer for our students who are already believers. They look to Christian adults to show them how to observe God's statutes and humbly walk with Him; don't miss out on this glorious opportunity.

Week 26 Day 2

I Always Need Him

I am the vine; you are the branches. If you remain in me and I in you, you will bear much fruit; apart from me you can do nothing.
John 15:5 (NIV)

I hate state testing season. I hate how it disrupts the week. I hate reading instructions, and I hate proctoring and walking around a tiny room for hours. But most of all, I don't like testing because I don't feel like a teacher. I don't teach at all. I don't even get to see my students. I feel like nothing more than a glorified babysitter with a teaching degree. Testing has its purpose, I know, but that still doesn't make me any happier.

One year, on the second day of testing, I fell into a dangerous trap. Because the day was mundane, boring, even trivial, I didn't start my day with the Lord. I thought that I didn't need to ask for help or wisdom since I was just administering a test that day. I thought, I'm just going to walk around the room and wait for the clock to run out. I don't need God, not today. Later in the week, when it is a typical teaching day, that's when I'll need help; I've got this—what a deadly snare from the enemy.

Jesus sets the record straight. He rebukes our illusion of self-sufficiency. In this verse, He does not say, "Apart from me, you can do fewer things than if you are in me." He says, "Apart from me, you can do nothing." Nothing means nothing. We are dependent on God for everything, not just ministry. We can't even proctor an exam in our own strength. My lungs can't keep breathing as I walk around the room, and my brain can't keep telling my legs to move without Jesus allowing it to happen. Every second our hearts beat is a gift from God. Apart from Him, we literally can't exist.

Shame on me for thinking my need for God was based on the difficulty of my day.

Every day I need Him; I always need Him.

Week 26 Day 3
Tutoring Time

I am the vine; you are the branches. If you remain in me and I in you, you will bear much fruit; apart from me you can do nothing.
John 15:5 (NIV)

As I have mentioned before, one of the most rewarding things about teaching is when students come back and show gratitude and appreciation. These moments confirm our hopes and prayers of making a lasting impact on our students and give us the energy to keep persevering.

I had one such email from a very bright student who did well on an AP exam and wrote to thank me. I was touched when I received the email with the subject line "Thank You, Mr. Way" and eagerly opened the message and began reading. However, I was struck by what he thanked me for. I thought he would thank me for all of the practice problems I had designed, or the speed at which I entered grades and handed back papers, or maybe the supplemental curriculum with lots of fun activities I wove into my instruction.

However, those did not make the list. The one thing that he was grateful for was simply the time I spent tutoring him after class. He thanked me for taking the time to explain to him challenging concepts. He thanked me for the time I took to sit with him as he wrote essays and give pointers along the way. He said that the time I gave him demonstrated my care for him and his future. It wasn't my teaching or content knowledge, but the extra time I gave him that made such an impact.

Wow, what a perspective realignment.

It's funny because every time I get a thank you note from a student, I am humbly reminded of what is important to students and how different it is from what I consider essential during the school year. Despite this pattern, I still forget. I still get too absorbed in the day-to-day. We need to remember that education is always about relationships. Above all of the trappings of the education system, your students need and most appreciate you.

Your time is the most precious gift you have to give- don't forget that.

Week 27 Day 1

We Submit Because We Love Him

Submit yourselves for the Lord's sake to every human institution, whether to a king as the one in authority, or to governors as sent by him for the punishment of evildoers and the praise of those who do right. For such is the will of God that by doing right you may silence the ignorance of foolish men. Act *as free men, and do not use your freedom as a covering for evil, but* use it *as bondslaves of God. Honor all people, love the brotherhood, fear God, honor the king.*
1 Peter 2:13-17 (NASB1995)

This level of submission to authority challenges me. Growing up in America, rebellion is celebrated. It was the brave patriots whose resistance to King George gave us our freedom. We are encouraged to emulate our forefathers. Submission is good, but only to a point. There comes a time when you must throw off your chains and fight for your rights. "Give me liberty or give me death." Grab your musket because "the British are coming!"

However, Christ calls us to a different life. He commands us not to rebel against authority but to follow His example of perfect submission. We are called to obey those in power over us, just as Jesus submitted to the Father. The Lord commands us to obey human institutions out of our love for Him. We show that we love the Lord by being subject to those over us. Scripture provides an all-encompassing description of all the types of authority we are to submit to. It is hard to find a medium of authority that does not fall under "every human institution." This means we are to be subject to our national, state, and city civil governments. We are to joyfully obey all as long as they do not go against God's law.

But the list doesn't stop there. We are also to submit to our school boards, principals, and instructional coaches. Any form of authority over us is to be respected. Again, we always obey God above everyone, but we are called to obey authority over us more thoroughly than most of us have been taught.

Peter here explains that this submission has a purpose. It is first motivated by our love for God. We submit for "the Lord's sake," and we "live as servants of God" (RSV). This means that even in honoring our authorities, we do not honor them above the Lord but respect them because we love God. We aren't trying to impress them and pay lip service. We need to show genuine respect. Even if we don't like our principals, we need to show that we love the Lord more. And out of our love for Him, we respect our principals. This radical call to submission is that by "doing good [we] can put to silence the ignorance of foolish people" (ESV). Our honoring of authorities proves our witness and advances the Gospel. This is a difficult mindset to adopt, but we can show greater respect to our leaders with God's help.

Respect your principal out of respect for God. Honor everyone because you love God.

Week 27 Day 2

Suffering Now, Glory Ahead

Therefore, we do not lose heart. Though outwardly we are wasting away, yet inwardly we are being renewed day by day. For our light and momentary troubles are achieving for us an eternal glory that far outweighs them all. So, we fix our eyes not on what is seen, but on what is unseen, since what is seen is temporary, but what is unseen is eternal.
2 Corinthians 4:16-18 (NIV)

These verses bring such clarity and perspective. I am so quick to become all-consumed by my problems. My frustrations compound, and I start to feel the weight of disappointment. Before too long, I become discouraged.

In my career, I have had classes that I could say I suffered to teach. Students that tried my patience and pushed me to love them when it wasn't easy or convenient. Like all of us, I've also been hurt by people when I was not in the wrong. I've agonized over the pain of being wronged and sinned against. Suffering demoralizes us until it consumes us. If we aren't careful, the pain of this sinful world can eat away at our souls.

However, we are not to lose heart. While every day is exhausting as you pour yourself out for your students, your inner self is being renewed. These real afflictions that press you down and make it difficult to wake up in the morning are not in vain. Each wrong that you experience is light and momentary compared to what is to come. Your tears of pain are producing an eternal glory that far outweighs your trouble. God knows that what you are going through is difficult, but these setbacks do not define you. Instead, they are refining you, and you will one day reap the rewards of such afflictions. Do not be overwhelmed by what is seen. Instead, fix your eyes on the unseen eternal glory your suffering is producing.

Take heart, Christian soldier, your battle wounds are temporal, and your future glory is eternal.

Week 27 Day 3
The Blind Wisdom of Fools

The wrath of God is being revealed from heaven against all the godlessness and wickedness of people, who suppress the truth by their wickedness, since what may be known about God is plain to them, because God has made it plain to them. For since the creation of the world God's invisible qualities—his eternal power and divine nature—have been clearly seen, being understood from what has been made, so that people are without excuse.

For although they knew God, they neither glorified him as God nor gave thanks to him, but their thinking became futile and their foolish hearts were darkened. Although they claimed to be wise, they became fools.
Romans 1:18-22 (NIV)

These verses help explain the spiritual warfare that we are involved in in the classroom. I remember a fascinating philosophy class where students were debating the existence of God. Surprisingly, most of them said that the physical evidence for a Creator was more significant than for the Big Bang. This admission of God's existence and His creation dominated the room. I sat there in awe. I never thought my students would say that God existed! Indeed, God is not hidden, but His invisible qualities have been clearly seen.

Then something interesting happened. When the knowledge of God changed from acknowledging Him as a Creator to acknowledging Him as Sovereign, as King, the conversation in class turned. Each student was adamant that God does not have the right to tell them how to live. They came up with all types of ridiculous reasons why even though they believed there was a Creator, they couldn't and didn't want to acknowledge the lordship of Christ.

They said that alternative universes could exist, denied the existence of absolute truth, and talked at length about extraterrestrial life. One student even proposed that we all lived in a simulated reality, and we can never know what's real at all. I could hardly believe my ears. My group of self-identified fact-based logicians was grasping onto fantasies in order to not submit to God and His law.

But I shouldn't have been so surprised since the end of these verses describes precisely this. Because they didn't thank or glorify God, "their thinking became futile and their foolish hearts were darkened." I had a group of fifteen students who all claimed to be wise, but their proud hearts had made them fools.

This experience and Scripture reminded me that the Gospel is not a debate in which we are trying to convince our students by scoring the last point to win an argument. Because they love their sin and are in rebellion against God, their minds and hearts are not objective. Their resistance to the Gospel is not a result of a failure on our part to be convincing but springs out of their own wickedness. Although God's existence is apparent, they don't want to submit to him. Because they love their sin, they resist the truth. As long as they value their sin over a Savior, they will never turn to Jesus.

Therefore, the remedy to see the kingdom advance is not for us to argue better but to pray that their hearts are changed and their blind eyes are opened. Until that happens, our students will always resist the Gospel.

It is beneficial to articulate arguments for a Creator and use apologetics, but don't forget that our students wear spiritual blinders that must be miraculously removed. Then and only then will they submit to the God Who has made Himself visible to all.

Week 28 Day 1
Spiritual Battle Alongside Students Part 1

Answer me, O LORD, answer me, that this people may know that you, O LORD, are God, and that you have turned their hearts back.
1 Kings 18:37 (ESV)

I always pray for the Lord to bring students for me to mentor and guide.

Sometimes, we support our students through the form of intercessory prayer. This is when you pray on behalf of a student for a period of time for a specific reason.

Later in my career, I had the pleasure of teaching in a private Christian school. I was permitted and encouraged to pray openly with and for students if they asked me. In late fall, a boy in one of my classes approached me and asked for significant prayer. The details aren't necessary, but he needed nothing short of a miracle. After he shared his request, I committed to consistently praying for him and meeting with him periodically to get updates. He thanked me, but his face was downcast. He wanted to believe that God would intervene but had already given up hope.

Later on, while in a time of prayer, I was reminded of Elijah's story and the showdown with Baal. I so often have read that story and skipped to the exciting display of God's power, but Elijah's prayer beforehand is crucial because it reveals why God intervened. As we see in Scripture, Elijah asked for God to intervene so that His people would be reminded of His power. A demonstration of His supreme authority would break their idolatry and bring them back into the welcoming arms of their Redeemer. Their hearts needed to be turned back to Him. God's intervention would be a catalyst to bring His people to repentance and back into fellowship with Him. This significantly changed how I prayed for this student and should change how we pray for bigger and better plans for them.

I still prayed that God would fix his impossible situation, but more importantly, I prayed that an answered prayer would be a defining, watershed moment for this boy. I prayed that God would turn this student's heart back to Him. That he would genuinely repent and that his love for the Lord would deepen.

Don't forget that our students need a strong prayer warrior in their corner and one who prays for their ultimate good, which is always closeness with God, and not just what they see as important.

Week 28 Day 2
Spiritual Battle Alongside Students Part 2
And when all the people saw it, they fell on their faces and said, "The LORD, he is God; the LORD, he is God."
1 Kings 18:39 (ESV)

As I mentioned yesterday, this time of intercessory prayer was very challenging and intense. Some days I agonized in my heart before the Lord and pleaded on this student's behalf. I have never before felt such a burden and solemn responsibility to pray for a student, and it was not easy. Some days I would forget altogether, and I had to redouble my efforts of discipline to keep my commitment to him. Thankfully, God gave me the strength to keep up the fight. I was also not alone. Several teachers and other members of our community joined together for months of fervent prayer.

Then, miraculously, God powerfully intervened and answered his prayer. I was so excited. Through months of no answer from the Lord, part of me wondered if God was going to act at all. I was so eager to talk to this student that I found out where he would be after class and rushed over to him.

After he told me all the details, I was thrilled, but I was even more pleased to hear him recount all that the Lord was teaching him through the process of waiting. His description of patience, peace, God's sovereignty, and the supremacy of his relationship with Christ was the real miracle and made my heart leap for joy and stand in adoration of the Lord. It is the Lord who changes hearts. Witnessing this firsthand and seeing that happen to a student in my class did wonders for my faith. I was so encouraged to see the Lord answer both the primary and secondary components of this request. He truly did the impossible. He both fixed the situation and fixed this student's heart. Immediately all of the months of labor in prayer were worth it. What an absolute privilege it is to approach the throne of grace on our students' behalf.

Pray confidently! God answers prayer, and He can turn your students' hearts back to Him.

Week 28 Day 3
Spiritual Battle Alongside Students Part 3

Then he was afraid, and he arose and ran for his life and came to Beersheba, which belongs to Judah, and left his servant there. But he himself went a day's journey into the wilderness and came and sat down under a broom tree. And he asked that he might die, saying, "It is enough; now, O LORD, take away my life, for I am no better than my fathers."
1 Kings 19:3-4 (ESV)

This part of the story always makes me scratch my head. Elijah has just witnessed one of the most prominent displays of God's power recorded in the Bible, but he then runs away in fear. He sinks into a depression that is so severe that he asks God to kill him. How does that happen? How could such a spiritual high lead to such a spiritual low so quickly? How could a prophet, of all people, become so disheartened?

These answers still elude me, but I have experienced this pattern after spiritual warfare. It was the strangest thing, but the day after hearing the incredible news of God's miraculous intervention in my student's life, I skipped my usual quiet time. The thought of prayer didn't even enter my mind the entire day. In the next few weeks, I struggled to read my Bible and pray. I wasn't focused on God during work and was very distracted all day. Then I became incredibly irritable, and bouts of sadness would overtake me. Worst of all was my neglect of personal growth with the Lord. In just a few weeks, I had grown distant. How could my heart have turned so cold? It seems so counterintuitive, but after seeing God answer prayer in a significant way, it was difficult to get back into the habit of praying for my students. After being in awe of God, it was harder to worship him.

I don't know if we are more susceptible to spiritual attacks after seeing God perform such a victory, or if we are satisfied that the prayer was answered so we aren't burdened to seek the Lord with the same zeal, or what, but this cycle is real. If Elijah could experience the mountaintop to valley experience, we all can.

Recognize the desire to rush to sin even after we have seen the might of our God. Be aware of this pattern and ask the Lord to help you navigate it for His glory.

Week 29 Day 1
Spiritual Battle Alongside Students Part 4

And the angel of the LORD came again a second time and touched him and said, "Arise and eat, for the journey is too great for you." And he arose and ate and drank, and went in the strength of that food forty days and forty nights to Horeb, the mount of God.
1 Kings 19:7-8 (ESV)

In this conclusion with Elijah, we see that the only way we are restored is through the intervention of the Lord.

This is something I did not do initially. After my mountaintop experience, I neglected my quiet time. I tried to heal from the exhausting spiritual battle through entertainment escapism or with friends. Day after day, I would watch TV or read, and day after day, I was not refreshed; I was not restored. I kept seeking rest but never really found it. The problem was that I was treating my spiritual tiredness as I would physical weariness. I kept sleeping in and napping and wondering why my soul wasn't being restored.

Finally, the Lord snapped me out of it and showed me that only He could replenish me. Spiritual exhaustion can only be healed through spiritual means. Physical healing, no matter how frequent, will never restore us spiritually. Afterward, it seemed so obvious, but at the moment, I could not see this correlation. We see this with Elijah as well. After his bout of depression, an angel intervenes and feeds him and restores him. God and God alone is the only way we will regain our spiritual strength after the battle.

Jesus is the Great Physician, and He is the remedy for all your maladies. Don't do what I did and run from the only One who can help. Take the angel's words to Elijah to heart. Your ministry as a teacher is still before you. "The journey is too great for you." Eat the bread of life and drink from the everlasting well. Find your strength in the Lord and carry on to the next mission.

Week 29 Day 2
Sow Indiscriminately
Then he told them many things in parables, saying: "A farmer went out to sow his seed. As he was scattering the seed, some fell along the path, and the birds came and ate it up. Some fell on rocky places, where it did not have much soil. It sprang up quickly, because the soil was shallow. But when the sun came up, the plants were scorched, and they withered because they had no root. Other seed fell among thorns, which grew up and choked the plants. Still, other seed fell on good soil, where it produced a crop—a hundred, sixty or thirty times what was sown. Whoever has ears, let them hear."
Matthew 13:3-9 (NIV)

There is so much packed into this parable. The most striking takeaway is from the sower. The sower does not discriminate where he throws the seed. This farmer spreads the seed (the Gospel) to all types of soil. He does not save the seed for the quality soil but plants it everywhere.

Often, I find myself waiting for the perfect moment or "right" student who I think will be most receptive to the Gospel. I believe that I can pick the ideal soil, and this will guarantee success. But I'm not the cause of the growth; God is. We must sow the good news to all, not just a few. Yes, sometimes the seed will not sprout, but our job is to be a witness, and God will cause growth.

Don't be stingy with spreading the seeds of redemption. Witness to all, trusting that seeds will find good soil and take root. Let God do what only He can.

Week 29 Day 3
Lives Worthy
Urging you to live lives worthy of God, who calls you into his kingdom and glory.
1 Thessalonians 2:12 (NIV)

We, as educators, understand the responsibility that our authority in the classroom and the community demands. We are aware that our conduct, even on the weekends at the grocery store, needs to be upstanding, just in case we run into a student. While this is excellent professional behavior, as Christians, we are called to an even higher standard. Therefore, we set our aim on our higher calling. We are to live our lives worthy not of our school's reputation or pride but for God. We are His ambassadors into the world, preaching the good news with our words and our example. We must be recognized not for our achievements but for being His children.

Dying to our reputation and belonging to Christ is not something to mourn. We sacrifice our honor but get the most generous upgrade imaginable. We are now associated with Jesus. We are co-heirs and co-workers. He calls us to work with Him in accomplishing specific things to further His kingdom. We are to be used by Him for His kingdom and His glory, not our own. We get to accomplish eternal things with and through Him. That is infinitely more than we could ever achieve on our own. How gracious He is!

Even the accolades of our career can never match the reward that awaits us. The world may reward us with a reunion of grateful students on our last day or with an excellent write-up in the paper at our retirement. While valuable, these experiences will eventually fade away. However, Christ is our ultimate reward. We get the privilege of being with Him forever. Being able to share in His presence and glory is a permanent and everlasting reward. We are treated the opposite of what we deserve as we sit at the table with our King. It is this heaven-focused mindset that motivates us to teach and live above reproach. No worldly acclaim or secular reasons for conduct can compel us more than our eventual eternal reward. Serve the King with joy; He loves you and smiles over you.

Week 30 Day 1
Seeing Growth and Fruit
Therefore, my dear brothers and sisters, stand firm. Let nothing move you. Always give yourselves fully to the work of the Lord, because you know that your labor in the Lord is not in vain.
1 Corinthians 15:58 (NIV)

I continue to be challenged, humbled, and comforted by this passage. I find that in my desire to see the fruit of my labor, I can sin. If I am not careful, I start to move beyond praying with faith into praying with expectation. This subtle difference is a slippery slope. When we pray with a demanding heart, we become prideful and assume that God owes us an answered prayer. We believe that this prayer will be answered because we're praying a good prayer. We assume that our prayers should be answered and answered in our timeline, according to our will and our purpose. But in doing so, our hearts are not humble but are instead saying, "I am wiser than you, Lord."

Next, as we continue down this sinful mindset, we find our satisfaction in seeing fruit. We overemphasize the fruit and downplay the act of serving. We are delighted to see fruit and devastated when we don't. We fluctuate in our joy by placing our hope in our own achievements and not in Christ alone. We can then find ourselves in despair and doubt. We wonder if God is even working at all, and we contemplate throwing in the towel. At this stage, the enemy has won.

We have to remember several truths and preach them to ourselves. God is God. He is way above me. His thoughts are not my thoughts, and His ways are not my ways. He will achieve His purposes, and any fruit will happen because of Him. Therefore, the timing of the fruit is entirely in His hands. He may, in His infinite wisdom, have fruit that occurs in thirty years. He could hide the knowledge of fruit from us for our entire lives. Whatever He decides will always be good and according to His will.

Only in His presence will we gain His perspective and marvel at His perfect plan. Any fruit we see in this lifetime is a blessing. We must humbly accept His sovereignty and wisdom. Seeing the fruit of my efforts is so rewarding. I often pray for the Lord to give me the blessing of seeing Him move in tangible ways among my students and in my school. But our hope is not in seeing the results of our efforts but in the action of Christ. Our worth is not based on our fruit. Our labor is not valued by tangible results. We are only called to work for Christ. If we do that, we honor and please God in our obedience. We can't let anything deter us from this glorious, eternity-shaping work. Don't lose perspective on how important working for the Lord is. Continue to give all of yourself to working for the Lord in your family, job, relationships, and everything you do.

We cannot see all ends and cannot possibly imagine the impact of even the smallest act of love. Therefore, we cannot lose heart but must persist even if there is no visible fruit in our labor.

If we labor for Christ, no labor is in vain.

Week 30 Day 2
Holy, Not Happy
He will sit as a smelter and purifier of silver, and He will purify the sons of Levi and refine them like gold and silver, so that they may present to the LORD offerings in righteousness.
Malachi 3:3 (NASB)

One of the most rewarding elements of teaching is the investment in our students' lives. We pray for those opportunities and wait in faith for them. We can even enjoy the unbearable days because we know that we are making tangible differences in our students' lives. This is what keeps us going. This is what keeps us in the classroom and not in another profession.

If you're like me, though, if you do not experience this feeling of fulfillment, especially for a long time, it is easy to second guess your decision to teach. Even worse, I started to question my worth as a believer since it seemed I was failing in my calling. I began to think, *if this; why does it no longer fulfill me? Maybe it's the classes I'm teaching?* Perhaps the kids will be better next year, and then I'll be fulfilled.

But this is faulty thinking. The truth is that despite being a fulfilling career path, teaching will never fully satisfy us. There will never be a year, let alone a week, in which we are completely satisfied with our jobs. And you will definitely have challenging years as an educator. Some years you may be able to count your happy days on only one hand. What do you do then? If we were called to teach, but it will not always make us happy, then what's God's purpose in calling us anyway?

We get the answer to this question in the verse today. God puts us in a refining fire to purify us and strengthen our faith. A refining fire is not a match lit under you; it is being put in the middle of a blazing fire. This fire burns and then removes the parts of you that are displeasing to God. Refining is not an enjoyable experience, but it is for our good. You will be tested and broken down to be built up even stronger. What if the classroom refines you and makes you more like Him? What if you were called to be a teacher not to make you happy but instead to make you holy? What if you are a teacher because it is the best way for God to refine you?

This is a sobering reality. God is so good to give us fulfillment and affirmation in our careers. But His plan for your life right now is not permanent happiness; that comes when you see Him face-to-face. For our time on earth, our most glorious good is to become more like Jesus. So, God uses our callings to kill two birds with one stone. We can both enjoy teaching and have it conform us into the image of Christ at the same time. In fact, when we least like teaching, I think the refining flames are the hottest.

Don't lose heart if teaching brings you to your knees. No career is perfect, but God uses every profession perfectly to achieve His purpose in you. Even though education is challenging, it is challenging for our ultimate good. We must always be conscious that our worth does not come from fulfillment or satisfaction on our worst and best days. Our real purpose is becoming more like Jesus every day.

Week 30 Day 3
A Needed Reminder

Here is a trustworthy saying that deserves full acceptance: Christ Jesus came into the world to save sinners—of whom I am the worst.
1 Timothy 1:15 (NIV)

Could there be a more clear and beautiful sentence in all of Scripture? Christ came to earth to save. Fully accept this truth. Don't let the enemy condemn you. Satan will often whisper, "You aren't worthy of God's love." This leads me to think that he's right and that I must somehow earn God's love. You can quickly spiral as you fashion an image of God in your head that's not the God of the Bible.

Paul reminds us that Jesus did not come to save those who were good or even decent but wretched, evil sinners. When Satan says that you are not worthy of God's love, it's true! We aren't, and God knows that as well. Guess what? He still loves us and died for us anyway. That's the Gospel.

I am so unfaithful to Him and thus often choose my sin over Him, and yet, it was in my rebellion that He died to save me and to save you. God is aware of our sin and has forgiven us completely. Such love and grace truly is incomprehensible.

Spend time today meditating on this reality in a spirit of gratitude. Give thanks to Jesus Christ for His death on your behalf.

Week 31 Day 1
Apologizing for Gossip
Here is a trustworthy saying that deserves full acceptance: Christ Jesus came into the world to save sinners—of whom I am the worst.
Proverbs 16:28 (NIV)

Warnings against gossip are abundant in Scripture. However, I did not fully understand the damage that gossip does until I had to seek forgiveness for it.

It was early in the year, and new staff members were settling into our school. Long story short, I was talking about one of the new teachers with some friends, and my comments dipped into the gossip category. I told a story about this new teacher that would cause others to view this teacher negatively. I was immediately convicted but kept fighting the feeling. I asked the Lord for forgiveness, and He did forgive me but reminded me that I had harmed a fellow believer and needed to reconcile and seek forgiveness from them. The Lord put this very clearly on my heart, but I knew it would be embarrassing and painful, so I kept delaying.

What would that person think of me? What if we could never mend the relationship? This was the worst first impression I could make.

Here's where the effect of gossip started to hit home. Because of my gossip, this person could have a negative, unearned first impression in other people's minds. This person wouldn't even get the chance to meet people without my story of them following wherever they went. I had sown division and caused conflict with my loose lips and sinful speech. I knew I needed to seek forgiveness but struggled to muster the courage to do so.

Finally, the Holy Spirit was swelling up in me so strongly that I had to get up and walk to this teacher's classroom. I had to shamefully knock on their door, walk over, look them in the eyes, and explain what happened. I don't know if you have ever damaged someone's reputation and apologized to them, but there is a hurt that is palpable in their eyes. I'll never forget that look.

I asked for forgiveness, and this person quickly forgave me. I was overjoyed but left with a real sense of the damage that gossip does.

Gossip destroys a staff and a community; don't allow yourself to fall into this temptation.

Week 31 Day 2
We Are Made Strong to Help Others

We who are strong have an obligation to bear with the failings of the weak, and not to please ourselves. Let each of us please his neighbor for his good, to build him up.
Romans 15:1-2 (ESV)

These verses apply to us in our churches and allow us to demonstrate our faith to our coworkers. Whether this is the end of your first year of teaching or you are a veteran, we have an obligation to help those in need.

When we are strong, we remember that it is a result of God's grace to us. We, therefore, cannot take out extra time or capacity and waste it on ourselves. We must use what God has given us to help those around us. We all know a teacher who is struggling and having a difficult year. Challenging students, health complications, or simple inexperience can all culminate and create a perfect storm in our colleagues' lives. Seeing someone we work with in pain should compel us to action. We should be filled with empathy and prayerfully consider how to help. Think what helping would do for our witness. How much would Christ's love shine through us? Think of how God could bless your coworker with your help. What if your help opens a door of opportunity to witness? The possibilities are endless.

Let us, therefore, build up our fellow teachers in whatever ways we can. This can be something as simple as helping an overwhelmed teacher grade after school one day. You could volunteer to help chaperone a sports tournament if one of the coaches can't make it. You could mentor a younger teacher or buy lunch anonymously for your admin staff. You know your school's needs better than anyone else, and with prayer, God will direct you to specific good works.

Thank the Lord for the strength He has provided you, and ask for His guidance in building up your fellow staff members this week.

Week 31 Day 3
God's Plan is Often Counter to Our Plan

You are my sheep, the sheep of my pasture, and I am your God, declares the Sovereign LORD.
Ezekiel 34:31 (NIV)

I am always surprised when the Lord moves in a way I didn't expect. Perhaps it is more accurate to say that I am surprised when the Lord moves in ways I didn't plan for Him to move.

For example, I remember in one class, I had been continually praying for an opportunity to address one outspoken atheist in class. I knew our discussion on free will would challenge her views significantly. I envisioned asking pointed questions and making her defend her different points of view. I had it all mapped out in my mind, all planned perfectly. I was thinking and praying that she would experience a breakthrough and would see Christ. By the end of class, I was confident she would be a confessing Christian. I committed wholeheartedly to this objective.

The class came, and I directed the conversation to play out just like I wanted. I was so proud of myself and eager to read this girl's paper and see her transformation. Two weeks later, as I was reading her essay, I noticed that her opinion had not changed at all. In fact, she was even more convinced of her atheism! I had utterly failed at converting her. All of my perfectly crafted questions fell short. I began to think that because I had failed, God wasn't moving in my classroom either. Then I read the paper of another student who I knew was a believer, but I hadn't gotten to talk with him about faith. He talked about how the chapter had increased his faith. He now understood God more deeply and was so excited to be growing in his knowledge of Christ.

Wow!

God was moving, and He answered prayer, but it was according to His plan and not mine. He didn't choose to break down the walls of an atheist this time but chose to increase the faith of one of His children. I immediately repented for assuming myself to be the master chess player, sure of the "right move" in God's kingdom.

We must not assume we know what our answered prayers should look like. We must always pray for God to move, and we should always rejoice in His movement, even when it isn't what we initially wanted or expected. We are His sheep, and He is the Shepherd. His plan is always perfect; ours is not. He is the sovereign Lord, not us.

Week 32 Day 1
Never Stop Humbling Yourself by Apologizing

Whoever conceals their sins does not prosper, / but the one who confesses and renounces them finds mercy.
Proverbs 28:13 (NIV)

I love this time of year because I get very comfortable with my students. I know their personalities, and it's easier to joke with them and vice versa. It's so nice to have routines followed and mutual respect established. However, with familiarity, I let my guard down with sometimes dangerous consequences.

One such occasion comes to mind. I was finishing up class with a special group of students. I had taught most of them for multiple years and in several subjects, so there was great familiarity between us. One of them was someone who hadn't turned in several papers and was barely passing. This student was brilliant but notoriously lazy. He could quickly turn in exceptional work but was easily distracted by other things. I'm sure you know the type of student I'm talking about. During class, the final exam exemption policy came up, which stated that any student with an A average did not have to take the final for that class.

A group of students was discussing being exempt with the student who had not turned in his papers, and they were teasing him that he would still have to take the final. He would be the only one taking the final as he was the only senior without an A. This was a private conversation that I overheard, and I wanted to exploit it to get a laugh out of the whole class. I joined in and started teasing that student in front of the entire class.

I told him that "he'd better bring his grade up because I didn't want to make a final just for him." As predicted, the whole class laughed, but he put his head down in shame.

I immediately felt convicted for teasing him so publicly. I had no right to use my power and authority to put him down, especially in front of the class. Nor should I have used his low grade to get a cheap laugh from his friends. Sadly, I kept fighting the conviction to apologize.

"I don't need to apologize to him," I tried to justify in my mind. I thought, He's tough; besides, it wasn't that bad. I even told myself that I saw him laugh, which wasn't true.

Over and over, I tried to talk myself out of it, but the Holy Spirit kept convicting me even stronger. After class, I knew I had to swallow my pride and be obedient to the Lord. I went to the student as he put away his things, looked him in the eye, and apologized. I felt miserable and was anxious about what he would say. I no longer cared about his assignments and grade but only wanted to restore the relationship I had sent a torpedo through. Thankfully he said it was okay and that he would do better about getting his assignments done. He packed up his bag and left. I stood there, frustrated at how I'd handled that situation. I let my desire to get a quick laugh damage a relationship with a student. I used my power to tear him down instead of building him up.

I still wonder to what extent he did forgive me. I pray that my mistake did not destroy two years of relationship-building with him. It was an incredibly humbling experience and a stark reminder that no laugh is worth calling a student out.

As teachers, we must never get so arrogant and prideful that we stop apologizing to students when we make mistakes. This is one of the dangerous consequences of unrepentant pride. When we don't confess our sins to God and others, it hardens our hearts to the Lord. This makes it harder to hear Him, and we lose intimacy in our relationship. The other negative result of pride is the damage to teacher-student relationships. Years and years of prayerful work with students can be destroyed in an instant. If we never apologize when we are wrong, we are not modeling our faith for our students. For it is even in our humility that our students can see that we are all regenerate sinners but sinners nevertheless, in daily need of the forgiveness of our Father.

Never be too proud to ask for forgiveness. Repent and receive mercy from those you wrong, including your heavenly Father.

Week 32 Day 2
Simple Evangelism

And he did not permit him but said to him, "Go home to your friends and tell them how much the Lord has done for you, and how he has had mercy on you."
Mark 5:19 (ESV)

Here Jesus cleanses a man of possession by a demon. It is such an incredible display of Jesus' power and authority that the man immediately wants to follow Jesus and is willing to do so. But then Jesus says something surprising. He tells the man not to follow him but instead to go home and tell everyone how much the Lord has done for him and about the great mercy that he has received. This man wanted to travel with Jesus, but God would rather he start spreading the good news in his hometown.

How many times do we expect our Gospel influence to look a certain way and don't even ask God if it is His plan for us? Maybe what my ministry looks like is not what I want it to look like. I often imagine what my ministry will be and try to chase my creation instead of listening to Jesus and starting with my family and my community. If we are always focusing on the next step or what could be, we miss out on what God has called us to do right now. While fixating on the future, we miss the present. Ultimately, it doesn't matter what we imagine our role to be; we are in danger of the disobedience of not evangelizing if we don't evangelize where God has us and in the way He has ordained.

So, what does evangelism look like? What news can

we share? Our story is the story of this man and every Christian. God has healed us from the devastating enslavement of sin. No longer are we bound to sin, sentenced to die separated from God forever. Instead, He has shown us mercy. Not based on anything we have done but purely by His lovingkindness, God has extended the most incredible, life-changing mercy on our behalf. In Him and Him alone, we have the forgiveness of sin. So, we are to tell all of those in our town this good news.

But spreading the good news is not just our testimony of salvation to unbelievers; it's reminding fellow believers as well. You share the Gospel when you remind your spouse after a hard day that God is our refuge, and He will give them rest. We encourage a coworker going through a trying time that God is good and is working all things together for good for those who love Him and are called according to His purposes. Don't confine testimony to your salvation, but share God's goodness with people in your daily life. What incredible deeds He has done for us. What great mercy we have received. How kind and patient He is. We should share this reality with all whom we come in contact. Don't wait one more hour; start sharing today.

Share with your family and friends all that the Lord has done for you!

Week 32 Day 3
Who the Son Sets Free

So Jesus said to the Jews who had believed him, "If you abide in my word, you are truly my disciples, and you will know the truth, and the truth will set you free." They answered him, "We are offspring of Abraham and have never been enslaved to anyone. How is it that you say, 'You will become free'?" Jesus answered them, "Truly, truly, I say to you, everyone who practices sin is a slave to sin. The slave does not remain in the house forever; the son remains forever. So if the Son sets you free, you will be free indeed. I know that you are offspring of Abraham; yet you seek to kill me because my word finds no place in you. I speak of what I have seen with my Father, and you do what you have heard from your father."
John 8:31-38 (ESV)

If you were like me and grew up in a Christian context, you may have heard the phrase "the truth will set you free" all the time. It is a famous verse that a majority of Christians can recite without any effort. I love its simplicity and its power. However, I have been so accustomed to it that I forget how radical Jesus' diagnosis is to the Pharisees. To better understand the severity of His statement, we can look at how the Pharisees responded. When Jesus tells them that those who sin are slaves to sin, the pride of the Pharisees rises. They are indignant and offended. They are not slaves. They belong to Abraham; they are free and independent! How dare Jesus say that they belong to anyone other than themselves. They are intelligent, privileged, and powerful. They are in control of their own lives and possess a status above the average person. The Pharisees rightly perceived that when Christ told them they were slaves, He was really saying that they were not strong enough or spiritual enough to save themselves. Jesus told them they needed a Savior, a humbling and humiliating message for them to receive.

I have found that this same sentiment is alive and well in the unbelieving hearts of our students. I once had a girl who spent most of the year adamantly defending her atheism. Then one day, she remarkably admitted that the world was too complicated for it to have happened by accident. She said that creation proves that God exists. I couldn't believe my ears.

Then, however, she made an even more shocking claim. She said that while God does exist, she didn't need Him. She had never needed saving. In every difficult challenge in her life, she had the intelligence, willpower, or money to get out of the situation. She didn't need a Savior because she could save herself.

Her pride struck me.

It reminded me so much of the Pharisees. She was not a slave! She was a privileged, smart, and talented student. She did not need saving because she didn't want to admit her total inability to obtain salvation. Furthermore, like the Pharisees, she didn't want to admit her inadequacy because she would then have to declare that God is on His throne, and she is not. Even though she acknowledged that He exists, she did not submit to His lordship, His rightful rule over all His creation. She did not want to submit to Christ, so she denied that she needed Him. How tragic.

Jesus summarized this perfectly: all who sin are slaves to sin. Apart from being born again, we can't do anything but sin. We must know that the sinner's heart is naturally against an overthrow of its authority. The sinner wants to remain in control of his or her own life. Understanding this helps us to cope when students reject the good news and helps us know how to pray for them. For it is only through prayer that their hearts will be changed.

Above all, it should also give us hope because Christ came to set the prisoner free. No rebellious heart is too hard, no chains too binding. And once those chains are broken, who the Son sets free is free indeed.

Thank God for His power over sin and slavery, and pray that he frees your students as well.

Week 33 Day 1
Standing Firm, Even if You Are Alone
Do not be overcome by evil, but overcome evil with good.
Romans 12:21 (ESV)

It was the last few weeks of school. I'm sure you know the feeling. You've worked so meticulously with students all year, and summer break is calling. Tired is an understatement. At this time, and in this state, I received news that there had been full-scale cheating on my final exam. I immediately contacted the principal, and we began investigating what had happened. After interviewing students, we had a better idea of the event and gave punishments, and that was that.

Then, parents became involved.

That week was one of the most intense and demanding weeks of my educational career. I was so busy. I had several meetings with students, constant emails from parents and students alike, and a two-and-a-half-hour conference with all parents, counselors, and the principal. At the end of the week, the most frustrating thing was that all of this communication felt in vain. Despite all the meetings and emails, both parents and students were not only dissatisfied with the punishment, but they didn't believe what they did was cheating. They were not convinced that they had cheated.

I heard all types of arguments, and all of them were

so ridiculous that I couldn't believe they were even suggesting them. And that was where the first seeds of doubt were planted. I was exhausted, why not just give in? Why not stop the whole thing, tell myself that they "learned their lesson," and move on? Why should I continue to hold the line when it was not working? What can you do if students did wrong, but they and their parents don't believe they did? And what do you do if you spent countless hours trying to convince them and you were unsuccessful? I was so tempted to cave, drop all charges, and say that they didn't cheat. It was more tempting than you might realize.

However, I knew I couldn't do that. Not only would I be backing down to parents when their students were in the wrong, but I would be blatantly breaking the student handbook in regard to discipline. I would be condoning unrighteousness. Thankfully, I had the backing of the school and the strength of God to stand firm. I knew that God had entrusted me with dealing rightly with students based on His standards and not the opinions of others. I also wanted to show mercy and compassion because the Lord has shown me nothing but grace. Therefore, I showed mercy in the punishment, but I still had to administer justice even if the students and parents didn't support me. It was a draining week, and my character was tested more than ever before. Now, I am even more convinced of the wisdom of honoring God by living His way.

We must stand firm in doing right, even without the support of students. Even when parents disagree with the definition of right and wrong, we must submit to God. Don't change your convictions based on students or parents. Instead, take confidence that God is the Judge of the world, and before Him we are held accountable and no one else.

Week 33 Day 2
In Hindsight, God is Working
Jesus replied, "You do not realize now what I am doing, but later you will understand."
John 13:7 (NIV)

Jesus is talking to His disciples about His forthcoming death, burial, and resurrection. At this time, they couldn't comprehend all that He would do. They were blind to His ongoing work right in front of them. It was only after the fact that they would be able to look back and see all that He was doing.

This reminded me of something that happened with a former student. God has been so good to bless me with encouragement from former students when I need it most. I received one such note recently, and it encouraged me more than some in a long time. The note was short and simple but demonstrated the massive impact the Holy Spirit has in our classrooms. It was also a needed reminder of how God is the Author of change in students' lives. I was shocked when I read his message. The former student told me that I taught him a lot about life and helped shape him into the young man he is now. He said that I helped him learn skills like time management and organization and that these things had drastically improved his high school experience.

I didn't know what to say. The way he remembered me was not how I remembered him. I didn't sit down and have regular meetings with him about his organizational skills. In fact, I probably should have been more intentional with him and more understanding. Usually, I just told him his backpack was messy, and he needed to stop losing the papers I gave him. That's it. We probably had more conversations than that but nothing memorable.

Even more puzzling was that I tried so hard to mentor this kid. Every day he came to my room during lunch and ate, so I had grandiose plans to pour into his life and help him throughout his freshman year, but he wouldn't have it. Each day I'd initiate conversation, and most days, he'd give a few-word response and put his headphones in. And not in a respectful way. Almost like a "Mr. Way, I only have thirty minutes to eat; I'm not going to spend them talking to you" type of way. I was persistent, but he never opened up.

Up until I heard from him, I thought that my relationship with him was a failure. But God reminded me that no work done for Him is in vain. I know that my interactions with this student were so limited that any impact came only from God. God was moving and at work; He did a work in this student's life. I can only rejoice and give Him all the glory.

Sometimes God opens our eyes and gives us a glimpse of what He was doing all along, and sometimes He doesn't. Don't be discouraged. The seeds we sow are still there, even if we don't ever see the fruit. God is always working and is doing a work more magnificent than you ever could. And that is how it should be so that He gets all the credit, fame, and glory.

Week 33 Day 3
We Are not the Conductors but a Stop Along Students' Journeys

Greet Prisca and Aquila, my fellow workers in Christ Jesus.
Romans 16:3 (ESV)

Greet Urbanus, our fellow worker in Christ, and my beloved Stachys.
Romans 16:9 (ESV)

Timothy, my fellow, worker greets you; so do Lucius and Jason and Sosipater, my kinsmen.
Romans 16:21 (ESV)

A few days before summer starts, I begin to reflect on the year. Inevitably, I start to wonder about the spiritual impact that I had on students. I hope and pray that they are one step closer to repentance and faith in Christ, but I never know for sure.

Sometimes my mind shifts from introspection to an unbiblical view of myself and God. I tend to panic and think that if they did not come to faith in my classroom, their odds of coming to faith later on are much slimmer. I think that I'm their best chance of coming to Christ. I elevate my importance arrogantly to think that I am the only one whom God can use to influence them.

This is wrong.

God placed you in your students' lives for an

incredible 180 days. You are only responsible for the time that you had. You are not the only one who can point them to Christ. You are not the only laborer in the field. Thankfully, your students still have professors in college, new friends, coworkers, future neighbors, and church members who will interact with them. Each one of us is playing our part. We are all co-laborers, fellow workers in Christ Jesus. We don't always see the impact of our contributions, but we can be confident that God is working out His perfect plan through His people. God will work out all things for His glory in the pursuit of His people.

There is hope for our students when they leave our classroom not because you were their teacher but because God is in control.

Rejoice that He had you play your part and trust Him with their future. We do not control their destiny, but He does.

Last Day of School: Final Prayer

For this reason I kneel before the Father, from whom every family in heaven and on earth derives its name. I pray that out of his glorious riches he may strengthen you with power through his Spirit in your inner being, so that Christ may dwell in your hearts through faith. And I pray that you, being rooted and established in love, may have power, together with all the Lord's holy people, to grasp how wide and long and high and deep is the love of Christ, and to know this love that surpasses knowledge—that you may be filled to the measure of all the fullness of God.
Ephesians 3:14-19 (NIV)

The last day of the school year is always so bittersweet. There is a real sense of loss in knowing that we won't ever teach these students again. We grieve not being able to see these students in our class again. Our students grow up in front of our eyes. Now, they are entirely different from who they were in August. However, we also look forward to much-needed rest and, if we're honest, spending time away from that one student who tried our patience every waking moment.

During this emotional time, I encourage you to contemplate all the Lord has done this year. Like at the start of the year, I usually walk around my room, past every empty desk, praying for students by name. Now I know them more. They are no longer names on a roster but pieces of my heart.
Could there be a more meaningful and powerful prayer for us to pray? Prosperity, blessing, and healing

are all temporary. However, there is nothing more eternally important than for them to learn of God's love for them, respond to His call, and continue to grow in the knowledge of God's love. I pray earnestly for their faith, families, and futures. I pray that the Lord will continue to follow them even though they will no longer sit in my classroom.

After I pray over each desk, I come back to my own and thank God for His help. My time of reflection turns into thanksgiving and praise. I remember all of the times He comforted me, gave me strength, and faithfully answered prayer.

I'm overwhelmed by God's power and that every good work was Him working through me. It's so humbling to know that we have the privilege of furthering His kingdom and His glory in our classrooms.

I then love to end the year the same way I began by dedicating the work that occurred in my room to the Lord.

Now to Him Who is able to do immeasurably more than all we ask or imagine, according to His power that is at work within us, to Him be glory in the Church and in Christ Jesus throughout all generations, forever and ever!
Amen.

Final Thoughts

Thank you for reading this devotional. I do pray that you have the tools and the mindset to teach as a Christian more confidently. I pray that your students see Jesus when they see you and that God will be glorified in everything you think, do, and say.

I always love to connect with teachers and hear about their struggles and victories. Please don't hesitate to reach out; I would love to hear from you at rightbeforethebell@gmail.com. I promise to read and respond to every email.

Thank you again, and I hope you enjoy your break this summer!

-Jacob Way

ABOUT THE AUTHOR

Jacob is a committed husband, father, and teacher. He has taught social studies for over eight years in both the US and internationally. He loves reading, watching movies, hiking, and serving in his local church. One of his greatest desires is to see teachers become all who God made them to be both in and outside the classroom. He lives and teaches overseas with his wife and two children.